Yes, You Do Have Time!

Learn to Capture the Small Moments in
Each Day to Complete Projects, Reach Goals,
and Build Income

James "Butch" Tanner

Dedication

I dedicate this book to my wife Carole, my daughters Jill and Kay, and my parents James and Martha Tanner. Thanks for your investment of love and encouragement in my life.

Table of Contents

Introduction

Just reading the title of this book may make some people frustrated. However, that is the reality—*Yes, You Do Have Time!* I personally understand your frustration very well. Even with years of time management experience, I still struggled to be able to get things done for myself. I was able to be productive for others, but not for me.

When I began to map out writing this book, my focus was on simple time management. The more I thought about it, the more I realized that neither I nor the people I was trying to reach with my message needed just a simple rehash of normal time management principles.

I knew that in a way those simple principles, no matter how well thought out, still failed to produce the time that I needed. As I talked to others, I found the same issues facing them. Those conversations and personal experiences prompted an entirely different direction.

I needed to develop ways that I could deal with major projects in small bites.

Like yours, my world is complicated. As a pastor of a large church, I work over sixty hours most weeks. Every day, I'm on call twenty-four hours. Many weeks, my "day off" is interrupted with members' needs. I plan something and then it gets changed, often at a moment's notice. An emergency can and does arise at any moment, rarely at a convenient time.

I clearly understand how people can say, "I'm just too busy," and be able to walk away feeling justified. I used to do that myself.

You have dreams, ideas, inventions, businesses yet to be born—all in your head. If you only had time, you could get those things out of your mind and into reality. Your dream would be able to positively impact numerous people. But, to be honest, right now you do not see yourself as having the time necessary. You may not even see yourself as even having time to read this book.

Take the time! If you don't, you will be missing one of the greatest opportunities to understand how to use your time in a way that produces tremendous benefits for yourself. In this book, I am going to show you how you can discover time that you already possess to make a huge difference. You don't have to rearrange your schedule, you don't have to come up with extra hours, all you have to do is rethink what you already have.

Throughout this book, I will help you by redefining the way you see just a small fraction of the time you have each day. As you read, I will help you identify "time debits" in your life so that you can avoid them.

In Chapter 3, you are going to go through a brief but powerful exercise which will help you discover the available Transitional Time that you currently have. You will also decide how much of that time you will invest in yourself. Later, we will walk through how to define your dream and learn how that plays an important part in using your time well.

In Chapters 6 and 7, we will walk through a number of ways to develop how you can maximize the use of your Transitional Time.

I believe that when you finish this book, do the exercises, and apply it to your daily life, it will truly revolutionize your world. You will become productive in ways that you never even imagined possible. You and others will benefit because of your time investment.

I know this because I've *lived* this. I want to show you how I have been able to capture small moments to make huge gains in my own life.

Entrepreneurs, business leaders, pastors, teachers, and any busy person who would want to be able to complete a personal project can benefit from reading this book. By approaching this book honestly, you will come away with a defined dream, a real plan on how to achieve that defined dream, and the time to make it happen.

What if I were to tell you that over 70 percent of this book was written in sections of time less than fifteen minutes each? And what if I told you that the entire project took less than forty days?

Well, both statements are true! Proof that the process works.

In this book, you will discover, that you do not need large blocks of time to make things happen. I promise you that if you move through this book and do the exercises, you will be equipped to meet your dream. You will be able to progress toward meeting any goal of any size. You will not have to produce one extra moment that you do not already have available right now. And in the end, you will be able to succeed.

Because I am a pastor, I want you to be aware of some personal beliefs that drive my thinking on time and its use.

God created each person with a purpose.
Each person is valuable.
Each person has something valuable to contribute in life.
God ask us to use time wisely.

Given the time to reach the goals that God places in your mind, you can dramatically affect your life and the lives of those around you.

Don't wait till tomorrow to start. Time is the only commodity that you can never earn more of or save for later. Every unused moment is gone forever. Learn to capture your small moments for huge gains. Let's start right now.

Get ready to reach your goals!

James "Butch" Tanner

Chapter 1
Time Redefined

Most busy people who struggle to complete personal projects and create new income opportunities do so because of a lack of time. I'm going to help you find the time by teaching you unique ways to invest in your time so that previously unproductive moments will pay off in a big way.

Everyone has the same amount of time. Whether you're the boss or the janitor, the chemical engineer or the delivery person, the one thing you all have in common is time. For years, you may have talked about, studied, and even followed time management principles. You understand that time management is excellent and necessary; it helps tremendously in the accomplishment of so many things.

In this book, more than just simply teaching you time management skills, I am interested in teaching you how to Invest In Time. Specifically, I would like to teach you how to use what I label as "Transitional Time" to create a totally different life.

In this chapter, we will take a look at time, the problem with it, and how to redefine the way you look at it. Additionally, I would like to equip you with new options so that you can have helpful tools to alter the way you think about your time. Ultimately, the desire is to create a time investment payoff.

Today, you and I both have 86,400 seconds to use. I have no more time than you, and you have no more time than me. That's 3,600 seconds an hour, amassing to an amazing 31,557,600 seconds a year. Wow! Put that way, it can seem rather overwhelming.

Zig Ziglar said, "The average person checks what time it is about three hundred times in a day. Yet, if you were to ask that person immediately after checking the time, they would be unable to tell you what time it was."

Time is extremely important. Or, put more accurately, the *use* of time is extremely important. Alan Lakein said, "Time is life." Every moment that passes is a moment we can never recapture. It is an opportunity—and missed opportunities can never be recaptured.

Ready? Let me help you understand how you can capture the opportunity presented by small moments to make huge gains.

A Problem Realized

Do you have dreams that you would like to pursue? Do you have debts you would like to pay off? Perhaps in the back of your mind there is an invention that you would like to develop. Is there time to get that accomplished? Just like you, I had those dreams, but couldn't find a way to get them out without making a huge investment of time that I did not have.

I cannot do everything, obviously, so many times I did nothing. I was swallowed up in the hugeness of what's going on around me and I felt insignificant. You may be just one of thousands of accountants, nurses, technicians, or whatever your trade is in the area where you live. You may see your value as less just because of the volume of people. And because of your perceived insignificance, you stop trying to achieve your dream. After all, you don't have any time to make it come true, anyway.

Hey—I want you to realize that you are much more valuable than you think.

You personally have knowledge and abilities that are important. You have the ability to add value to your family, community, church, and work. Don't miss the opportunity to learn how to do that. By learning to invest in time, you will learn to accomplish much more than you ever thought you could.

The great part? You already have the time!

I know—my story is probably much like yours. I would want to get in shape, write a book, drastically reduce my debt, etc. ... you know the drill. Common but seemingly unreachable goals. The issue was time. When did I have time to do that?

Each year I would declare that this was the Year of the Great Opportunity. I would set new goals and declare that they would be reached. But it wasn't to be. Once I got off track with my first goal, the other goals would quickly fall apart also. Like dominoes.

Each year ended the same: I had been overwhelmed by work and didn't accomplish my goals—again. My multitude of ideas would go unshared and lives would go unchanged because I was stuck in my own definition of time.

One of my greatest needs was to get out of financial debt. And every year I would make a pledge to do everything I could to accomplish this. I am a fan of Dave Ramsey; he does a great job leading people on the journey to become debt-free. Often I would listen to his show and get practical and helpful ideas. I went through Financial Peace University and began to take the baby steps. I established an emergency fund (which has been a lifesaver more than once). I was able to pay off a portion of my debt successfully, but I continued to struggle to achieve being debt-free. We sold most of the things that we could sell. We downsized our house. We drove older cars. But we never could seem to break free of that ever-present debt.

It always seemed that major unplanned expenses were there to push us back into the debt trap. Maybe you have experienced some of these: unplanned major medical bills, car repairs, appliance repair, house repair, care for extended family, or a job layoff or change. These, in addition to the normal bills, tithes, and extracurricular and education expenses for children, make the vicious cycle seem unbreakable.

One thing in particular that frustrated me was when Dave would say, "Get a second or third job temporarily." At the time, I was working all I could to get ahead in a salaried job with no overtime. Work was overwhelming. Because of the nature of my job, being on call twenty-four hours, I couldn't just pick up another regular part-time job. My wife worked outside the home and we used almost all of her income to pay off debt. I felt trapped.

The freedom of being debt-free seemed to be so slow in coming. I began to believe that I had no other option than to just slowly grind things out and suffer through years of painful, debt-strapped living.

My belief was based on valid data—something you may relate to. I was consistently working over sixty hours a week and on call twenty-four hours a day.

Many times I have planned a project and started it, only to be promptly interrupted because work calls. It's hard to have productive plans when you can't plan from one moment to another. My solution was to stop setting goals and avoid the disappointment of another failed year; however, with my personality, I still found myself dejected.

How many of you, like me, have turned to time management in hopes of finding a solution? To use my time well, I researched and read over twenty books and dozens of articles on the subject. I became very good at applying time management principles. As a result, I've written papers on time management and led several groups through training. Yet this book is not about time management.

There are many wonderful books out there to help you in that area. Surely we will touch on some basic principles, but only that. What I found is that even with every moment accounted for and used, I still had no time to write or do many of my personal projects.

I have learned from my personal experience and that of others that it is possible to be well organized and active but fail to reach your goals. That is where I was: totally frustrated and feeling like there was no way out.

Have you been there? No time and little hope of accomplishing your dream?

I had no time to invest in my dreams, either ... or so I thought.

A New Discovery

A new discovery truly changed my life. I hope that I can help you make this same discovery in your life.

I become aware of the powerful results of the effective use of what I label "Transitional Time." These are not huge blocks of time and they are not periods of time where I have to reschedule to make the time become available. Transitional Time is already a part of our daily routine.

How to View Time

Time is an investment. When you look at time, I want you to see it as an investment you make every moment of every day. Those frustrations I had while progressing through Dave Ramsey's material gave birth to this idea. Just as he had talked about wisely investing funds, I began to think about time in that same way. Time invested wisely will produce a positive return. If I see time as money, then I want to know the best way to invest it for the maximum return. The time investment principles you learn in this book will help you accomplish that goal.

Time is here to be used for our benefit, not just managed. We need to utilize our time to its greatest benefit. There are events in life that are not worth the investment of our time. Some events in life require both a good management of time and a good investment strategy in time. Learn how to recognize where time is best invested and where it is best managed so that you can receive the greatest benefit.

In redefining how you view time, I want you to think about what you are putting into the time that you have. Are you considering your time as extremely valuable? Are you making sure that your time investment is a good one? Have you considered asking what your investment in time is paying you back?

You need to understand what I just said: a good investment in time will pay you back.

In the process we will go through together, I do not want you to be concerned with making sure that every moment of every day has something happening in it. That's a cultural trap that we have fallen into. We teach our children from a young age that every moment has to have some activity, every moment must be filled with productivity. During the school year, we have numerous extracurricular activities and we applaud the child for participating. During the school breaks, we enroll them in camps and clubs and any other activity that will keep them busy. Unfortunately, we are building into them an idea that *activity* is *productivity*. We have even brought that idea into our own minds. We have come to believe somehow that activity itself is achievement.

It is not!

Do not confuse being active with investing in your time.

I want to teach you how to invest wisely in the time you have. You cannot make more time—you will always have the same amount of it as everyone else— but you can change how you invest in it.

I began to see a significant change in my life when I looked at how I used small blocks of time. As I viewed those blocks, they were already filled with activities that I could not change. The activities were necessary according to the demands of my work or my routine of life—but many times they did not require a great amount of mental involvement. I began to view these activities as being Transitional Time.

I will repeat these words many times throughout this book. Read closely:

Transitional Time is any time I am moving between two tasks where I personally have control of that time; when I am doing a routine task which does not require constant mental attention.

During Transitional Times, I think through the process that I will show you in this book. In utilizing this pattern, I have discovered the time I needed to achieve my dreams and complete my projects was always there. I just couldn't see it. Until now.

I want to help you see it also.

You can utilize your mind to improve your income status and relieve yourself of debt. Wouldn't that be worth it? Instead of constantly saying that you don't have time, effectively using your Transitional Time will allow you to be creative enough that you can create additional income so that you will be able to do more with what you have. I could not do a traditional second or third job to produce extra income—but I could use my Transitional Time to launch a new opportunity.

In your Transitional Time, you could come up with a solution for a problem at work—perhaps by providing a service or product that your company does not currently offer but customers are requesting. This could fill a valid gap, even get you a promotion. You may spin off a new business. You could produce additional income and be able to pay off your debt—then you can allow your children and your family to have the vacation that you've been wanting. Or even just a nice dinner occasionally.

Personally, for years I was on such a tight budget that I felt guilty for just eating a nice supper out. There should not be any guilt in that. We work hard and also prepare most of our meals at home from scratch. So to be able to go and eat supper occasionally should be okay. Yet in our mindset it wasn't, because of our finances. Getting out of debt makes such things much easier.

I want to encourage you to use your Transitional Time to create additional income sources. Your idea is worth improving and marketing. Don't just assume that because you know something, everyone else is aware of that information already. There are numerous streams of information that people do not know about. If you can develop a product, a teaching module, or a coaching opportunity where you are able to teach someone else something you already know, you both could benefit. The Internet opens up numerous opportunities to teach something you have mastered via video and online courses.

Dream a little. If you put together a course that people needed, charged a small fee, and did the class several times a year, what kind of income will that bring in for you?

You do have the time you need to produce whatever is necessary to reach your goal. Much of that time is available to you in Transitional Times. Actually, about 70 percent of this book was developed by using eight- to twelve-minute segments of time. You have those same time segments available to you.

Over the time that we are together in this book, I want to help you to be able to discover for yourself just how powerful Transitional Time can be. In the next few chapters I want you to be able to discover your Transitional Times, define your dream, map out your plan, and develop specific ways that you can effectively utilize your time. I want to help you reach your dream. So push ahead to the next chapter, where you will learn about "time debits" and discover how to turn them into credits!

Chapter 2
Ditch Time Debits

Everything does not deserve your time investment! You must invest in time wisely or it will bankrupt you. I want you to be alert to these ten time debits. Certainly while reading this chapter, you will think of others, and I encourage you to write them down for yourself. Remember, your goal is to be able to have small amounts of time throughout the day so that you can think about your projects. We will address some specifics on how to successfully use your Transitional Time to complete your projects in Chapters 6 and 7. Properly and promptly dealing with time debits will prevent them from robbing you of valuable moments.

Since you are now looking at time as an investment, you definitely do not want to waste it. You want to make sure you effectively invest in every moment you have available. When you are able to do something that is productive with your time, call that a *credit*. If time is spent, and the gain is negligible, call that a *debit*.

Right now, I am going to be focusing on time in general and not just specifically on Transitional Time. However, many of these time debits that will be discussed will limit the amount of useful time that is available. It is good to understand the overall picture of your time debits, in order to effectively gain access to the time needed to complete your projects.

Potential Time Debits

I believe the greatest time debit is not having a defining dream to follow. Chapter 4 is fully dedicated to understanding and pursuing your dream. You don't want to miss what you will learn there—it is life changing.

I have personally experienced each of these time debits, and you will relate to most of them as well. These debits are eating away at you and deducting from your available time throughout the day. Let's look at a few of them and see how we can turn them from debits to credits.

You may want to use a chart like the one below to help you think through how you will build a winning strategy to turn each one of your debits into a credit. You can download a copy of the below form from www.timeinvestor.net.

My Strategy to Turn Time Debits into Credits	
Debit (negative)	Credit (positive)
1. Schedule	*I plan to take charge of my schedule. I will not completely fill every minute so that I can properly deal with emergencies. I will schedule time for myself and my family.*
2. Procrastination	*I will break my larger goal into several smaller ones.*
3. Interruptions	*I will learn to say no to some interruptions and ask that time be scheduled to deal with some of the other ones.*

- Debit: Scheduling

Or, more accurately, the *lack of proper scheduling*. You need to make sure that you are properly scheduling your day so that you can more effectively utilize the moments. One poor scheduling habit is not choosing to do the things that require the most mental input at the time of day that you are the sharpest to be able to complete the task. It may be that everyone else can do the particular task that you're talking about at 9 a.m., but for you, it may be better that you do it at 1 p.m. or 7 a.m.

Think through your day. When are you the sharpest? That's when you need to devote your time and mental energy to tasks that take a lot of thought. Doing the wrong task at the wrong time can lead to a significant waste of time.

Do not over-book your schedule and do not over-promise. Your schedule should never be completely full. You need to have time built-in for emergencies or a change in plans. Rarely, in my life, does everything go according to schedule. If you don't have some flexibility built into your day, then everything has the potential to collapse. A full schedule often produces a lower quality of output because you do not have time to rethink or evaluate.

Block out a time just for you somewhere in your schedule. I remember the first time that I ever did this—I felt guilty and thought somehow I was cheating. Later, I discovered how significantly important that time was to me in order to be more balanced and productive. You do not have to feel as if it's inappropriate. You need time to recharge. Schedule it.

+ Credit: Proper Scheduling

Proper scheduling with personal time blocks included can be established. No over-scheduling, no over-promising. Set a schedule that allows you to meet the demands of the day and exceed the expectations of those around you.

- Debit: Procrastination

Mark Twain remarked, "If you have to swallow a frog, don't look at it too long. If you have to swallow two, don't swallow the little one first." Many times when we see something as a problem, we avoid it—as if avoidance is going to make it go away.

Problems only get larger or more complicated when we ignore them. Sometimes, in the business world, our problem goes away in the respect that we lose a customer, then it becomes larger because we've lost our source of income.

Procrastination is a habit that is absolutely fatal to effectiveness.

The major reasons for procrastination are:

1. Unclear priorities
2. Poor organization
3. Hesitancy to risk
4. Boredom
5. Exhaustion
6. Potential conflict
7. Overwhelming tasks

Which of these issues is making you ineffective? The reality is that if you act on something quicker, you have the ability to be more effective in the long run. Take the issue that is stopping you from acting and deal with it. Whatever you fear, face it. Don't spend your time worrying because worry itself is a waste of time.

You could accomplish much more if you take the time that you spend on worrying and instead spend it thinking through a problem and working toward a solution. Celebrate your victories but move on. Don't hang around in your defeats either.

Procrastination is primarily a bad habit. My definition of a "bad habit" is *something which continuously steals positive energy for negative results.* You have the opportunity to save time that you can invest to pay off positively if you decide to stop procrastinating. Utilize your schedule and your best time for energy and get the task done.

+ Credit: Replace Procrastination with Action

Here are four things you can do to help take action:

1. Identify the most important task to do first. If it happens to be the worst one for you, remember Mark Twain.
2. Break the project up into smaller pieces.

3. Establish unmovable but realistic deadlines for each piece. Do not allow these deadlines to be moved. If you do, you are in danger of falling back into old bad habits.

4. Celebrate your progress and then celebrate the completion of the project.

- Debit: Interruptions

It's important for you to be able to distinguish between that routine interruption and those which are important. You need to know whether or not something is wasting your time.

Here are some questions to determine whether or not some interruptions are valid.

- Is it actually something you are responsible for?
- Is it something that needs your direct supervision?
- Does it impact the project that you are currently working on?
- Can it be delegated?
- Is there another person who is better capable to answer the question?

- Can you give someone else the information and authority to answer the questions?
- Are there clearly written instructions to follow?
- Does the person interrupting actually listen to the response and act on it appropriately?
- Is the person interrupting in fact a procrastinator?

When dealing with individuals, it's important for you to learn their personality type. If they are relational, then spending a brief time talking and discussing is very important and may not be considered a time debit. It may be a motivational building moment.

The relational side needs to happen quickly. Then, move directly into the problem-solving side or information-giving side. You need to direct the conversation quickly and effectively, while at the same time building the value of that employee or person who is the interrupter.

Interruptions cost time. For every disruption that you have, it takes about five minutes to regain your focus on what you are doing. These unexpected interactions deduct minutes from your productivity.

Five minutes doesn't sound like a lot, but over a course of a day with twelve interruptions, you've spent an entire hour just trying to refocus. Unproductivity! To put this into perspective, let's think about it this way: if you are losing sixty minutes of productivity every day, in a five-day work week you are losing five hours. In a fifty-week work year, that adds up to 250 work hours lost just in trying to regain your focus. That is the equivalent of thirty-one eight-hour working days.

A five-minute interruption may not seem so problematic, but it can add up to six weeks of unproductive work time. Wouldn't you rather have more time—that is, *productive* time—so you could benefit in other ways? How many hours could you have to put toward your own goals by simply reducing the number of interruptions?

+ Credit: Limit Interruptions, Deal with Them Quickly

It is impossible, not to mention unnecessary, to stop all interruptions. It is also very important to be able to stay on task. One of the things you can do to stay focused as you are interrupted is to write down words which will remind you of your thought process. If you are in the middle of reading, you may want to highlight a spot on your report or computer.

Another thing that you can do is segment your day. Try to make all of your phone calls at one time. Choose another period to write and answer emails, letters, notes, or memos. By working with a good schedule, you can allow people to know when you are available for questions. They will respect that.

- Debit: Anger

Anger steals energy and moves you away from your goal. When your anger is directed toward someone else, your focus is no longer your goal. You are now focused on them. At that point, they are in control, even though many times they are not even still in the room. With a word or phrase, attitude or action, they can easily get you off track, sometimes for hours. Don't give them the benefit of knowing that they have that kind of control over you.

Anger messes with your emotions and restricts your thinking ability. Creativity is shut down and your vision becomes cloudy and nearsighted. You become sidetracked and unproductive.

Take control away from anger and spend your time focused on what is important to you—your goals. Take the time that you would normally spend boiling in anger, and move that energy into being productive. It will take you time to learn how to redirect your emotions, but it is invaluable to do so.

+ Credit: Focus on the Dream

When you feel anger rising up in you, step away, think about your dream, and focus all your energy on dealing with issues related to your goal. Don't let issues build up between you and someone else. Make sure you deal with each issue as it arises, quickly and appropriately.

Deal with the person in the same way you would want someone to deal with you. Handle them with care and respect. Move the focus of your attention to your project and do not dwell on your anger.

- Debit: Worry

Worry is very inventive, but in a negative way. It has never stopped any event from happening nor solved any issue. Worry wastes a vast amount of time, having us think about things that many times have never happened before, nor will happen in the future.

Worry has never changed anything—planning has. Worry can produce an ulcer; proper planning can provide excitement and energy. Any project needs to be reviewed realistically so that objections or problems can be overcome; however, worry does not provide solutions. It is important for you to turn your energies in the right directions.

Don't spend your time dealing with issues that are not in your control. Spend your time developing solutions for your project. You can give instruction, research, and guidance, but you can't control the outcome.

+ Credit: Work With What You Control

Focus on the areas you are in control of and take charge. Don't worry about events that are happening outside of your control. When worry does arise, turn to producing solutions.

- Debit: Failure to Delegate

If you have the ability to delegate a task, do it.

The old adage, "If you want something done right, you have to do it yourself," is *WRONG!* All the proverb proves is a lack of investment in developing the people around you to do the quality of work that you expect.

Answer this: why should someone invest their time in learning how to assist you, if you are never going to allow them to do so? There are times when the appropriate person to do the task is someone else. Work to develop the people around you into highly qualified and competent team players.

Perfectionism often prevents delegation. Don't hang on to your task and try to make it perfect.

My definition of perfectionism: *just one person's personal preferences that seem less than perfect to others*. Really! How many times have you seen someone else spend hours on something to get it perfect, only to discover an imperfection within moments of them presenting their project? Or, even worse, maybe the results were not even liked at all?

Remember, many things are subjective; it is based on personal feelings, tastes, or opinions. There are as many opinions as there are people. In the church world, the joke is that for every three people, there are at least five opinions. Don't get lost in perfectionism. Set a clear picture of a goal and allow people to utilize their unique skills and talents to reach that goal.

Another issue with delegation involves meetings. It is not necessary that you make every meeting once you have clearly established a group's purpose and goal. As a matter of fact, there are some times when the work could get done better if you sent a letter or a memo rather than being there personally. Sometimes when you are in the room, a team of people that you are working with fails to be creative. Of course that's not true of all meetings, but just consider it, and skip the meeting when appropriate.

+ Credit: Delegate With Clearly Defined Tasks

Clearly define the task result expected, with checkpoints and deadlines, and delegate it to the most skilled person for that task.

- Debit: Meetings

Business leaders consider meetings as the fourth largest waste of time and a major contributor to ineffectiveness. A poorly planned meeting is even more wasteful.

In today's world, meetings can be done in multiple ways. You have the ability to meet with anyone, anywhere on the globe, in a video call that can be brief and to the point. The Internet offers a variety of platforms to conduct meetings. Clearly written documents can be sent out ahead of time. Questions about those items can be sent back to you so that you can have answers to the questions when you meet.

Counterintuitive but true nonetheless, the longer a meeting goes the less productive it becomes. A meeting should have a clear agenda that can legitimately be handled in the time frame established for the meeting. There should be a definite beginning time and ending time.

If you choose not to begin the meeting because someone is not there at the beginning, others will immediately see the meeting as unimportant. They will also see that you do not value their time. They showed up on time—don't waste it. Even if someone is not there, start the meeting on time. If that person is consistently late, it may be necessary to replace them. Most often, people arrive when they want too.

Do your best to end on time, or, better yet, early. It would be better sometimes to send people on their way, let them think through the issues, and come back together for a brief meeting, or email responses to specific questions, than to continue to go on.

In the 1980s, time management trainers emphasized that if a meeting were not worth someone giving up a hundred dollars to attend, don't have the meeting. Today that would equate to three hundred dollars. Time is money, but unlike money, it is irreplaceable. Use the time you have wisely.

+ Credit: Develop High Value Meetings

Only require meetings that are of high value. Have a clear agenda. Begin and end on time. Be informed and prepared ahead of time so you can contribute to the discussion and increase the value of the meeting.

- Debit: Emails/Mail/Texts/Voicemail

Modern technology offers many wonderful opportunities for remaining connected to people without face-to-face conversation. However, you need to remember that being connected does not mean that you have actually *communicated*.

Most of these technological advances do not allow you to see the body language of the person. According to communication studies, 80 percent of communication is nonverbal body language. These non-personal methods of messaging can sometimes cause more problems because they are unclear, and a single written sentence can have multiple meanings.

Modern methods of messaging also create massive interruptions. These breaks reduce the useful time in a day dramatically. Unless you are in a crisis situation, schedule a time of the day that you will respond to emails, mail, texts, voicemail, and other forms of messaging.

I have found that many of the messages that I have received throughout the day are actually something that someone else needs to handle. I usually take a short time, just before my breaks, to glance through the different types of communication and answer any of them that can be brief or need a response right away. For the remainder, I have set aside a time in the afternoon which works best in my schedule specifically to respond to them.

Everything is not urgent. Most often, the urgent is not even important. It is not necessary for you to interrupt your work to communicate with someone about a frivolous matter.

Establish a daily time that you can read and respond. Read email or mail and deal with it at that moment. If a response is necessary, do it then. As a rule, never read your mail twice. It is usually a waste of time. Remember, you want to become a time investor. You have a dream—somewhere you're wanting to go, something you're wanting to do—so don't waste your time.

+ Credit: One And Done

All communications are dealt with daily. People receive the answers they need and you are not overwhelmed with responses to make later.

- Debit: Social Media/Gaming

People can literally spend all day on social media and gaming. Don't be one of them. If you want to be a part of social media, schedule it on your calendar. It does not even have to be a part of every day. If it is a part of every day, establish a specific amount of time that you will spend there and then shut it off. Gaming should be treated the same way.

Here is one incentive that can help. Call a plumber or general maintenance person in your area and ask their rates for a job that only takes a quarter of an hour. Apply these charges to yourself for your social media or gaming time.

+ Credit: Limit My Time On Social Media

Limited exposure allows you to catch up with a few people or have a short time of relaxation and is not allowed to rob you of your time to invest in yourself.

- Debit: Decision-Making

The inability to make a decision is a principal reason for failure. When a problem or question arises, make a decision. Act on it. Don't get caught thinking it must be perfect. Robert Schuller said, "You don't have a problem—you just have a decision to make."

It is interesting to note that US Army officers are advised that when in danger, any action, no matter how poorly conceived or poorly executed, is preferable to no action at all. They know the important thing is to do something. They also know that if they are stuck in indecisiveness, it could cost them and the people around them their lives.

The same is true for you. When you don't act—you lose. Other people around you lose as well.

These thoughts can help you in decision-making:

- Don't over analyze.
- Clearly identify the facts.
- Consult other qualified people.
- Don't try and anticipate everything.
- Don't be afraid of making the wrong decision.

+ Credit: Make a Decision

Make a decision; it gives you a direction to go. If it turns out to be a poor decision, then make another one.

Time Debit Consequences

Time debits rob you of your full potential. You have the ability to achieve great things. Don't let time go untapped because it has been wasted.

If you regained an hour a day because you properly dealt with many of the time debts, you could be much more productive. Work could be achieved in a faster time frame. Opportunities could be grasped. Challenges could be met.

But what are some other consequences? If you don't deal with time debts effectively, you lose the opportunity of spending time with your spouse, you miss the chance to spend time with your children, and you miss opportunities to just have fun. Your hope could be to go have fun skiing, playing tennis, or doing some hiking in the mountains. But many times, you do not do things like that because you don't have time.

Realize that if you are allowing time to be wasted, those time debts are robbing you of much more than money. You have more important things to do. Wisely budget your time.

Another consequence is in the income bracket. Why should you get a pay raise if you are a low producer? Why should your boss look at you as someone that needs to be promoted to the next level, if you are not able to produce at your current level? It may be that the reason someone who was hired after you gets looked at first for promotion is because they're better investors in time. You may look at other people and simply say, "If I had the time that they did to get those things accomplished, I would also."

In reality, you have the same amount of time and many of the same opportunities all around you. If you were to actually look at those people's schedules, you would find out that they are jam-packed. But even with their packed schedule, they consistently make time for themselves, their families, and their passions.

Moving Forward with Better Control

Now that you have learned how to ditch some of your time debits, you should be able to have a little more time on your hands. In fact, you have a lot more time than you think you do.

I want to help you recognize the opportunities you have, learn to invest in your time, and grow personally. As you continue reading, you will be excited when you walk through the discovery exercise in the next chapter. You will discover the time that I have talked about. *Your* time that you already have. Small amounts of time that you can invest to produce huge gains.

Yes, you do have time! Come on, let's see how much time you have!

Chapter 3
Discover Your Transitional Time

Transitional Time is one of the most powerful discoveries that you can make. Finding time to which you did not think you had access is a tremendous boost to your confidence in your ability to be able to complete a task. Time also gives you the greatest opportunity to be creative.

In this chapter, I will help you discover that you have more time to invest in yourself than you think. You will see firsthand an experiment of mine which completely revolutionized the way that I thought about time. The results were amazing. I encourage you to do that same kind of experiment for yourself. Others that have tried it have shared their own amazing results with me. So keep going. You are about to make an amazing discovery.

One of the best tools you will use to discover your time is the Day Map that I will introduce you to at the end of this chapter. The power of this one activity to find time in your busy day is nothing short of stunning. Remember, you are not looking for large blocks of time to put toward a project—you are learning where to find those short segments that I label Transitional Time. Later in Chapters 6 and 7, you will learn how to use that time effectively. As a result, you will be well on your way to success.

Yes, you have more time to invest than you think!

Skeptical? I was. My time was booked solid. In my normal busy schedule I struggled to meet the demands that I had to achieve each week. There just was no more time to be had.

After years of missing opportunities, failing to reach goals, and saying it was because I did not have time, I had conditioned myself to believe it. The problem wasn't my time—the problem was that I had conditioned myself to believe the wrong things. I struggled to see things any differently.

What you believe is powerful. Your beliefs may be holding you back, just like mine were holding me back. By the end of this chapter your beliefs will have changed. You will see that you really do have time to invest in yourself to accomplish your dreams!

Eye-Opening Experiment

I did a test to see what I could do in a ten-minute walk by recording what I said while going to work.

The test didn't start out so well, because for the first hundred yards, my recorder wouldn't work. But I didn't give up. I had a goal! Finally, it began to respond. With the recording underway, I wanted to see what could happen while I walked to work. This was my first test, and it was unrehearsed and unplanned.

It went like this:

Testing one, two, three.

What can you do in a ten-minute conversation with yourself on your way to work? That's the question, especially when you don't consider ten minutes to be a very long time. Every morning I walk to work, that is about the time it takes. On the way I pray, greet people, and think through the daily schedule. Today, for instance, is a Thursday. I have study notes to finish up and plans to make for a small group training tonight. I've already done my homework for the training but I'll need to go back over all that material so it's fresh in my mind. As I walk along, I can't be continuous with my recording because there are so many different things I need to be careful of. I won't be talking when I cross the street, nor am I recording when I'm greeting other people. It is amazing, though, how many thoughts and ideas you can get into print in this short walk.

Imagine that you were wanting to complete a writing project. You may write as if in a journal, or think about designing a "how-to" book, or you may want to create a pamphlet to promote your product or business. One of the best things to record may be to just put down random thoughts that are coming to you that can help you in different projects. You will be amazed at how much you can get done by putting thoughts down during that ten-minute walk.

Yours may not be a walk. You may be going by way of a car, bus, or subway, and as such you may have a thirty-minute drive or ride. You can listen to inspirational things to boost your self-confidence and your understanding. You can listen to a book being read to you and increase your knowledge on a particular subject—if you stay focused on one subject area, and are listening each time you ride or drive, you will soon have a tremendous level of understanding and expertise in that area.

You could even alternate between listening on one trip and writing thoughts on another. If you're like me, you are traveling back and forth to multiple locations numerous times during the week. Even if you took 50 percent of these opportunities, the amount of ideas that you could continually put down on paper would explode.

Always have some method of putting down your ideas. A memo pad to physically write on, memo notes in your phone, a voice recording, or any other way that works for you. Don't lose the ideas of the moment. Little things add up.

At this point, I'm a little over halfway to my office and I am getting ready to cross a busy intersection. In Hong Kong, China, one of the things that always amazes me is that most of the crosswalks only allow you to cross half the street at a time. So I'll stop recording for a bit and make sure I get across safely.

One thing good to do before you walk, drive, or ride is to lay out an outline of some things you would like to consider. This outline doesn't need to be large. As a matter of fact, having only a couple of ideas to think through may be all that you need to focus on. By having an outline to prompt your thoughts, it can help you be more productive in a lot of other things as well.

One of the statements Chandler Bolt made in a video that I recently listened to really stuck with me. He stated that if he hadn't written his first book, he would have left more than $17,000 lying on the table that was there to get. How much are we leaving on the table? What are we not accomplishing that we should be? It is not a matter of having too little time, because everybody has the same amount; it is a matter of utilizing what time we have, to make a difference.

During this brief ten-minute walk, I have not talked the whole time. There have been several periods where I've stopped to take care of other things. But this is just a brief example of what can happen on the walk to work. Have to go now. I've arrived at work. I hope this brief exercise has helped you understand that you are able to accomplish much more than you sometimes give yourself credit for.

The Power of the Experiment

Realizing what could happen on this ten-minute walk launched this entire project and completely altered the way I would approach time. It is interesting that in my brief walk, with nothing preplanned or rehearsed, I was able to put down 750 words. Had I had an outline of ideas before I left the house, these could become much more focused. If I were writing a book with 25,000 words, then I could simply do it in thirty-four trips to or from work. Those ten-minute segments equal five hours and twenty minutes.

Doesn't that fact spark your interest? What can you accomplish that you never thought you had the time for, just in writing during a ten-minute period of time that is already designated to another purpose?

See, investing time in yourself does not mean that you have to take time away from your already busy schedule to be able to accomplish significant progress in other areas. This discovery was one of the most freeing things for my creativity. Soon you will find that this type of investing will produce dividends that begin to pay you back.

Looking Forward

Stop looking back at your failures. Look *forward*. You are committed to growth and achievement. You may have suffered from the consequences of poor time investment in the past, but not after today! You may not always have control of your income directly—you can't always determine your work schedule—but you are always in control of your Transitional Times.

Remember what Transitional Times are? Those are your travel times; lunch and other breaks; your waiting-in-line time; waiting on the doctor, dentist, or lawyer. Literally any time that is in-between can become usable Transitional Time. Times that can be of dual use can also be considered Transitional

Time. The more you use your time, the more you will discover.

Amazing results began to occur in my life from the very first day that I took advantage of Transitional Time. It amazed me how much could be done. I can remember times when I even felt cheated that I didn't have a trip coming, that I didn't have to be in the car for thirty minutes to an hour.

Simply by investing minutes, you will literally save *hours*. During those minutes you can start a new business by developing a business plan and model in your head and putting it on paper. Over a short amount of time, it can become a well-thought-out launch. You can write a book and completely change the way people view your topic and you. Others will begin to see your value. You can use those times to study and become an expert in an area that you really want to work in.

The answer is not always working harder. Your aging body will only last so long, after all. There are only so many hours in a day that you can spend awake and working. So the key is learning to invest your time in places that make significant long-term differences.

Let's face it: many of us go to a job that controls us for the entire work day. If we let it, our job would even control us outside of work hours. We may long for a time when we can simply do something more. We want to be free from the boss's demands or the bickering of the employee. We want something more!

Decide to give work your best effort, so that the hours you dedicate there are productive. But just as importantly, decide that your work is not going to control your life. After all, one day you will retire or be laid off or fired; you don't have to be under the complete control of someone else. Look forward to the future and take the steps to make it become the reality that you want it to be.

Yes! You Can Invest in Time Wisely

There is hope! Time investment is a skill that you can learn and it can be acquired by even the busiest person. You can learn to invest in time and profit from it. Time usage is extremely important. You don't have control of a lot of it, but small amounts will work. You must commit to take control of the time you do have. Make it have a big payoff.

Recently, *The Atlantic* magazine reported that the average American spends the equivalent of nearly one work week stuck in traffic every year. The average one-way commute to work in the USA is twenty-three minutes; in Beijing, China, it is fifty-two minutes. Other sources report that the average person in the US and Europe spends approximately forty-five to sixty minutes every day waiting in line for something.

As you can see, there are plenty of opportunities to invest in time.

Small time investments can be found in many places. What about the time it takes for your computer to turn on? What about using one of your break times specifically to develop your idea? If you are a mom or dad taking your child to school, this can be time spent building your children, encouraging them, and leaving them with the desire to be with you again. After you drop the kids off, instead of just kicking back mentally and relaxing, why not turn on your creativity and focus on one of your goal areas for just a few minutes?

Get the kids involved. Ask them to give you suggestions before they get out of the car. After all, kids are naturally creative and imaginative.

For example, I read an article recently that revealed the findings about what you could do with just a single paperclip. Three different groups of people were given paperclips and asked, "What can you do with this?" One group came up with over a hundred ideas. Neither of the other two groups even came close: one had less than fifty and the other less than twenty-five.

It is interesting to note that the group that got the largest number of responses were kindergartners. The other two groups were school-age children in middle school and high school. Kids see things differently than adults, even young adults. They might not have the answer, but they may spark the answer. Don't miss that opportunity!

The Power of Small

My parents encouraged me to begin investing in a retirement plan when I was eighteen. The investment began with very small amounts and it seemed like I was not getting anywhere very fast. Over time, though, my investment grew substantially.

Your investment in time is the same way. If you regularly invest in small amounts, you can actually track your investments and experience the excitement of seeing the growth of ideas and opportunities. I will be giving you a Time Investment Ledger in Chapter 7 that will help you do this effectively. Your attitude about your time and what you are able to accomplish will dramatically change.

The significance is sometimes missed, until one day you wake up and realize that the momentum has picked up and is pushing your goal forward. Then comes a magical day. You look at your investment and you realize that it is paying you back for all the time you've invested. You have more time and more opportunity than you ever did before—all because of your wise investment. Luck and good fortune did not produce this outcome—wise time investing did!

Quality time invested in yourself is never a failed venture.

Routines in Chaos!

"Chaotic" can sometimes describe the dramatic changes in my work schedule. You may recall that my schedule can change every day and that I'm on call twenty-four hours a day. Routine is sometimes hard to come by. However, I find that I can still build routines in certain places of the day.

Every morning, I make sure that I'm up early. For me, this seems to be the best time, because it has the least interruptions. You may find a different time works better for you. Your goal would simply be to find somewhere that you could build a routine.

In those first moments of the morning, the tone of my whole day is set. The first thing I do daily is read; I read several chapters of the Bible. The second thing I do is spend some time praying, because I want to ask God to give me guidance through the day. The third thing I do is exercise for eight minutes. (That is not a lot of exercise to start with, but I do walk to work and that is about all my routine allows in the morning. I found that without exercise, I have less energy in the day. My focus improves when I exercise.) While I eat breakfast, I scan the news. Before I leave for work, I review the plans for my Transitional Times (I will give you steps to laying out good plans in Chapter 5). With that little bit of a routine, it gives me the opportunity to be more creative.

Discovering Your Transitional Time

Day Map

The Day Map (available under tools category at www.timeinvestor.net) is critical to changing your mindset. You may be like me: I had convinced myself that I was stuck in a life that was under the control of everyone but me. This exercise will help you discover that you have control over more time than you previously imagined.

Before you do the map, reread how I defined Transitional Time.

Transitional Time is any time I am moving between two tasks and I personally have control of that time; when I am doing a routine task which does not require constant mental attention.

Many different activities can be considered Transitional Time. Some of them include:

- Driving/Riding
- Riding the bus
- Subway
- Walking to work
- Waiting for an appointment
- Standing in the checkout line
- Dusting the house
- Mowing the yard
- Walking the dog
- Break time
- A few minutes after your lunch break

There are ninety-six quarter-hours in a day. Each box in the Day Map represents fifteen minutes. Choose a normal day and indicate how you use each block of time in that day. Use a highlighter to identify the blocks that you have some control over what you do during those minutes.

In each block that is highlighted as being in your control, place a number indicating the minutes you control in that fifteen-minute block.

You can make it simple by marking W for Work, S for Sleep, L for Leisure, E for Eat, and so on. The goal of this exercise is *not* to make sure that every moment is filled with activity. The goal *is* to identify the areas of the day that you have personal control over.

12 mid				
1 a.m.				
2 a.m.				
3 a.m.				

4 a.m.				
5 a.m.				
6 a.m.				
7 a.m.				
8 a.m.				
9 a.m.				
10 a.m.				
11 a.m.				
12 noon				
1 p.m.				
2 p.m.				

3 p.m.				
4 p.m.				
5 p.m.				
6 p.m.				
7 p.m.				
8 p.m.				
9 p.m.				
10 p.m.				
11 p.m.				

Now that you have done a Day Map, you should be much more aware of time that is available to put toward your project. The amount of time that you potentially have available probably surprised you. I know when I first did this exercise, I was astounded at the minutes I discovered.

How many quarter-hour blocks did you discover you have some control of? _____

How many minutes in a day does each of those blocks total? _____

How many of those minutes would you be willing to invest in your own dream? _____

Minutes I am willing to invest: _____
Number of days each week: _____
Multiplied by 52 weeks: _____

Total Potential Investment this year: _____

I imagine that you just found out that you have an amazing number of minutes that you can put into developing your dream this year that you did not think you had before the exercise.

You have just made some significant discoveries about your time as you have done the Day Map exercise. Now you want to learn how to focus the time that is in your control and make it work for you. In the next chapter, we will be looking at the most important part needed to successfully launch your project or idea.

So let's get to the business of making the time that you discovered *productive*.

Chapter 4

Develop Your Dream

You Must Know What You Want for Your Investment to Matter.

Dreams define life. Moving through the exercises in this chapter will help you learn how to discover, define, and defend your ambition. With a clearly defined dream, you can consistently move forward, overcome obstacles, and succeed at reaching your target. When you successfully invest your time in your dream, you will positively change your life and the lives of others around you.

In Proverbs 29:18 (KJV) it states, "Where *there is* no vision, the people perish . . . " So true! Not only do you need to have a dream, but you need to understand how to define that dream. You can be a dreamer and have a number of good ideas, but not have your thoughts clearly defined enough to achieve any of them. A clear definition is important to the entire project. Without that, nothing else can happen.

You will have a clearly defined dream by the time you finish the exercises in this chapter.

Investing your time in an area that doesn't help you reach your goals is discouraging. Doing so constantly will lead you to believe your dream is impossible to reach and grant you the right to give up. When you stop pursuing your dream, you are condemned to sit on the sidelines and watch life speed by.

Charles Lamb referred to a dreamless person's career as having three periods:

1. The time that they will do something in the future.
2. The time that they could do something, if they acted.
3. The time that they might have done something, if they had focused.

You are determined to define your dream. Quality time investing will drive your vision forward because it is focused on your dream. The dream gives the clarity needed to make real progress. Results will produce happiness, contentment, satisfaction, and achievement.

You will not have the results of the dreamless. You are not going to be a "could-have-been-great" person. You will have a defined dream guiding you. The results of your life will be staggeringly different.

With vision giving you a purpose, your career's three-period scenario will change to:

1. The time that you had the promise to do something.
2. The time that you grasped the opportunity and did all you could.
3. The time that you pursued making a significant difference to the end.

In the end, this will lead to a life fulfilled.

Nearly Panic Time for Me

What is your dream? If I were standing beside you right now and asked you to define your dream, could you?

I was startled to find out several years ago that I could not articulate what my goal in life looked like. All of a sudden, it dawned on me that the reason why I could not reach my dream was that I could not *define* it.

Let me repeat: the reason why I could not reach my dream was that I could not define it.

I nearly panicked! As I struggled to define it, I realized that the vision wasn't even clear to me. When I understood that I could not even get a clear picture of my sense of direction, it became even scarier. How do you define something that you can't even nail down? In the busyness of life, I had misplaced my dream.

Not knowing your personal life direction is, unfortunately, quite a common thing. Many people wander through life without ever having an idea of what their purpose is or what would truly make them contented.

You may have a clear picture of where you want to go, or perhaps you lost your direction along the way. Either way, don't skip the exercises of this chapter.

You may not do them all, but at least do enough to clarify your dreams. They are vital to effectively invest your time.

Although you may think it's a waste of time to plan out and think through your dream, the opposite is true. One of the greatest wastes of time is traveling in the wrong direction. You may have great ideas and even great opportunities, but if you're going in the wrong direction you're going nowhere. Once you discover that you've arrived at your non-destination you will end up having to backtrack through months and possibly years of effort. Your investment of time in all that period could potentially end up wasted.

Don't wait to look back over your life and discover your wasted efforts. Plan out your life so that you know where you are headed and can make wise investments of your time along the journey. Remember, progress made in the wrong direction is not progress at all.

Again, take the time to define your dream. To fail to do this step will setup opportunities for failure at many different stages. You can prevent that downfall and replace it with success by having a defined dream.

Personal Passion/Discovery

The first task to complete with your Transitional Time is to spend time discovering your dream. What are you passionate about? Do you like to hunt, fish, or boat? Do you like ballet, opera, or musicals? Do you like to read books or short articles about specific subjects? Ask a friend, "When you're around me, what am I most often talking about?" You may think you know the answer to that question, but your friend may shock you with their observation. What are your ultimate goals? Begin to ask yourself what you can do, during your time investments, to accomplish a small piece toward that dream.

Where do you envision you will be five or ten years from now? Where do you want to be in the next twelve months? Most people think of the future as being so far away that there is no need to plan for it right now, yet the opposite is true. If you do not plan now to take the small steps that are necessary to shape the future you want, it will never arrive. The future you arrive at without following a personal plan will be somebody else's plan.

Time does not naturally flow to productivity, unless it is focused to fulfill a dream.

1. Focused time is guided by your passion and dreams.
2. Focused time engages itself in productive tasks.
3. Focused time tends to remain in your personal control.
4. Focused time tends to stay focused on the project and does not see the need to rush off and deal with every crisis.

When you know your passions and dreams, your time investment will move to achieve them. That becomes the natural outcome of properly invested time.

Dream Insight (Three-Phase Exercise)

Phase 1: Quick Responses

Answer these questions. Over analyzing is forbidden (this is meant to be a brief exercise). Be honest. Consider that everything is possible. Just give the first serious response that comes to your head. Just think about what you would do and write it down quickly. Don't take too long. You will have more time to think about it a little later.

1. What would you do if you just inherited five million dollars?

2. If you could live anywhere you wanted, where would you choose?

3. If you could work in any field, what would it be?

4. If you were given the next three months off, with pay, for the purpose of improving your skills and learning about anything you wanted to study, what would you choose to focus on?

5. If you had the opportunity to redesign the community where you currently live, what are three things that you would definitely like to change?

6. If you could put your beliefs on five billboards and you are limited to five words on each one, what would your top five beliefs be? (Don't worry about getting the five words for each billboard. Just one word or phrase to define each belief will do for now.)

7. If you had one million dollars to give away to a worthy cause, which cause would you choose?
8. If you lost your current job, what kind of work would you want to do?
9. What is your "someday"? ("Someday I will do/start/become/etc.")

Phase 2: Why?

Hopefully you enjoyed dreaming a little with those questions. Now, I want you to go back and look at each of these questions again and take a little more time to answer the question, Why? Why did you choose that answer? If it actually came true, would you be excited or satisfied?

When I went through this exercise, I found that several of the answers I originally put down were not the answers I stuck with, after considering the "Why." One example is where I would live. The place I'd chosen has beautiful falls, cool summers, great opportunities for family ... but is brutally cold in the winter! At this point in my life, winter is something to go visit, not where I want to live. So my answer changed.

During this phase is also the time that you can develop the five-word billboards of belief. I think these defining beliefs may be the most important thing you will write down. It is the foundation upon which all your dreams rely. Apart from your strongly held beliefs, your dreams will fade away. So make sure you give this one a little extra time.

The reason I limited it to five words is that it is easier to write something out in long sentences than in short statements. A limit of five words requires more thought. I want you to be able to be brief, concise, and clear. If anyone were to walk up to you and ask, "What are your beliefs that power your dream?," you should be able to reply easily and with authority.

As you walk through the "Why" portion of this exercise, feel free to change your answers if you discover doubts. Once you have the "Why" question completed, it will help you review, revise, or renew your original response.

Phase 3: Reconsider

Go back to the questions one last time. Consider your original answer, then the answer you chose after the second part of the exercise. Answer the following questions:

1. What answers did you change in Phase 2? Why did you change the answer?
2. What answers did you not change in Phase 2? Why did you not change the answer?

Through the three phases of this exercise, you have been walking through the discovery of the basis of your dreams. Also, you got to check your goals against your values. Dreams can only survive long-term if they match up with your beliefs.

Elimination (Exercise)

The elimination exercise is simply making a list of things you are certain that you would *not* want to do. To eliminate options is a valid way to begin to hone in on what you really desire to do.

The Power of 3 Minutes (Exercise)

Write down your dream. Do this with a pen and paper.

1. Set a timer for three minutes.
2. Once you start the timer, write down single words and short phrases, as fast as you can write, that give all that you know about your dream.
3. Do not stop for an entire three minutes. If you get stumped or run out of ideas, write down anything that comes to your mind that further defines who you are until the full three minutes is up.
4. Once you have finished this three-minute drill, review what you have written.
5. Put the related ideas in a group. As you group them, you will discover some important things begin to surface.
6. Circle or highlight those things that excite you. Don't be afraid of changing what you originally set out to do.

Once you have determined those few things that excite you, begin to think about which one is most important to you. Ask, "How does that impact my life? How can I personally become more involved with this? What can I bring to the table that will allow others to see the value I offer?"

Defining the Dream

Last year I had the opportunity to address a university classroom filled to standing room only. I asked the almost-seventy students in the room if they wanted to be successful. Every hand shot up and there were verbal confirmations coming from everywhere.

Next, I asked three of the most exuberant students to tell me what would define success for them. None of the three could give a reply. Success was indeed wanted—enthusiastically—but no one could tell me what it was. For the next forty-five minutes I shared with them how to define their own personal success.

Briefly, we discussed that:

1. Your definition of success determines your dream.

2. Your definition of success must be built on your personal values.

3. Your definition of success must be yours—you own it, and it belongs to no one else.

4. Your definition of success must have defined goals which are able to be developed.

You need to write down your dream and check it against your definition of success; only then will you be able to reach your goal. Dr. Gail Matthews, a psychology professor at Dominican University in California, found that you are 42 percent more likely to achieve your goals just by writing them down. Simply by writing it down, the level of commitment rises. Having a clear destination stops you from leaving the future to chance. The defined dream gives you the essentials needed to make the planning produce meaningful results.

Your dream is like a puzzle. You may be doing a fifty-piece puzzle or thousand-piece puzzle. Don't let the inability to see the whole picture at the first frustrate you. Unlike a puzzle, you can't determine exactly how many pieces it will turn out to be.

So, don't get caught up in the speed at which you work it out. Take your Transitional Time and work on it. Your work is more like that of an artist, you are creating something and adding to it, or taking away from it, as you go along.

Brainstorm (Exercise)

During the course of a day, make a list of all the dreams you have discovered that you want to achieve. Leave nothing off the table when considering options. Ask yourself, how do these dreams already connect with you? How do they fit with your current:

- Hobbies?
- Talents?
- Exceptional skills?
- Tools or situations you like to work with?
- Environments you enjoy working in?
- Things you are passionate about?
- Problems you hope to solve?

Give yourself about thirty to forty-five minutes of time to write this down. Walk away from your list for at least twenty-four hours.

After twenty-four hours, when you come back to your list, ask these questions:

- Would I be willing to give my time to this dream?
- Is this dream something I would truly like to accomplish?
- Is this dream something I would like to define my life?
- Which of these dreams are most important to me and I would truly regret if I didn't do them?
- Is there a dream listed that I could abandon and not feel badly about?
- How do I help others by fulfilling this dream?
- Is now a good time to pursue this particular dream?

As you go through this stage, there is a natural sense where you begin to realize that some of the dreams aren't really important. Eliminate those for now. Of the dreams that are left, prioritize them.

Choose your top three dreams.

Now take three pieces of paper and place one of the three dreams you chose at the top of each of those pages. Define the goal of each dream as clearly as possible in one sentence. Usually it is more difficult to make a clear, well-defined statement, the fewer words you use. Be patient, be brief, and be clear. The results can be powerful.

Begin a brainstorming session about each of these particular dreams. Record everything you can think of that would relate to that particular dream. Also, write down all that you need to have to accomplish that dream (education, new skill, finance, health, etc.). Do this for each of the three dreams.

Once you've done that, review each of the three, and honestly assess if that dream fits you. Are there parts of the dream that you're just unwilling to do? Based on your own personality, which dream do you prefer? In light of your thought process of the last twelve months, which of these are you more passionate about? Write your responses on each of the three sheets.

Walk away for another twenty-four hours and continue to think it through. During this twenty-four hours, you may want to do some research on each of the three areas that you've brainstormed about. You may even want to go beyond that twenty-four hours before you come back to the list, but try not to go more than forty-eight hours without returning. Avoid getting caught up in the need to do a lot of research and make sure that it is exactly the right fit. You can never know all you need to know before starting anything. Don't let the unknown stop you.

When you come back to the three lists, review them and update any new information about the three dreams. Now think about these questions:

- How will fulfilling this dream affect the way I spend my day?
- How will it impact my family?
- How will this affect me financially?
- How will this affect my health?
- Am I willing to take the small steps to plan it well and make it successful?
- Am I really passionate about it?

After reviewing these three, which one will you choose? Your choice will provide you positive boundaries. These boundaries will help you be able to stay on track. In choosing to pursue one of these dreams you are saying, "Yes, these other things would be fun, possible, maybe even profitable, but I am focusing my energy, planning, and resources on this one area so that I can pursue my passion and live my dream successfully."

Prospective Investor (Exercise)

Imagine that an investor approached you tomorrow and said they had the ability to fully fund you and your dream project. The only requirement they have is that you must give them a very detailed and clear outline of your proposed business project seven days from now. Would you be able to have a clear enough picture to earn their support? If you have to come up with that dream in seven days, here are some things that you may want to consider.

1. State the dream in one sentence.
2. Who are you helping or what problem are you solving by reaching this dream?

3. How much funding would it take to get your idea active?
4. How many people need to be involved?
5. Answer the basic Who, What, Why, When, Where, Which questions.
6. Describe whom you will market your idea to, how you plan to do it, and your proposed pricing.
7. What are the similar ideas and products out there, and what sets you apart from them?

Use these questions to write out a business proposal to inform your prospective investor.

Originally, I struggled to move forward because I could not define my goal. I did exercises similar to the ones you just read about (and hopefully did). Through that process, the dream became clear. Life became focused. Free time began to show up. And my time became an investment that began to pay me back in many ways. By defining my dream, I defined my win. My dream now defines my success and it guides my life.

Defending

A dream is powerful. It is a guiding tool. Many of the time debits can be overcome by focusing on your dream. It gives you the ability and desire to overcome the issues that are going to arise. It will also give you the ability to face the Dream Killers.

Dream Killers tell you it is impossible to achieve your goal. They will let you know that there are more qualified people to do your project. Eagerly, they tell you that others are better writers, researchers, inventors, developers, and speakers than you. Constantly, they share that there are numerous reasons to stop pursuing your dream.

What they do not know is that your dream is now defining your life. It is giving you purpose.

Edward Lindaman encourages us to dream by reminding us, "It helps to realize that everything that is now possible was at one time impossible."

It is your dream! Don't stop just because someone else thinks you should. After all, a vast number of inventions and solutions out there were met with

major resistance. Don't worry about the resistance—
sometimes it just means you're on the right track.
Every day you will meet opposition. That's okay.

When you are focused on your dream, moving
through resistance is easier. You see progress that
others don't see, because you know your goals. They
don't know your direction, because they don't have
your dream. Let your dream define you.

Don't waste your time worrying about what a Dream
Killer says. Evaluate what they say. If there are valid
points to consider, use the information to your
advantage and allow their negative comments to
become something that benefits you. But don't get
caught up in mentally arguing with them or trying
to work through all their issues. Don't allow them to
distract your focus and your energy away from the
project. Remember you are targeting your goal and
your definition of success.

In the end, the best defense of your dream is its
completion.

At this point in our journey, you know what Transitional Time is. You are aware of time debits and know how to turn them into credits. You have discovered an amazing amount of time to focus on fulfilling your dream. Now you are able to clearly define your dream to anyone who asks, including—most importantly—yourself.

All this information is significant, but the power to produce is in your ability to plan it out. Good planning leads to positive results. As you prepare for the next chapter, get ready to learn how to plan the use of your valuable time to get life changing results.

Chapter 5
Plan Well for Wise Time Investment

Decisive planning makes your time investment pay off big.

Planning is critical to the success of any project. It brings life to your dream. At this point you realize that you have a significant amount of time that you can dedicate to your project. That time is in your control.

Now planning will make that time go to work for you.

The plan does not have to be highly complicated or intricate, but it does need to give you clear guidance toward reaching your goal. Your plans will help you get where you want to be.

A dream or goal defines where you are going, but a plan gets you there. In basketball the goal is defined by putting a round ball through a round hoop.

Nothing else scores. But it is a set of designed plays that gets you through the opposition and allows you to score. In football, it's getting the ball into the end zone. Again, if you don't cross that line, you don't score. And once again, there is an opponent trying to prevent you from scoring. If you do not score, you can never win. A good plan will get you in the end zone to score.

Every game has a goal in order for it to be successful. So does every dream! Your decisive plans will help you capture the small moments and allow you to score and win. Your goals give you something to aim for and keep you centered on where you need to be. With them, you spend your energy wisely.

Brian Tracy gives some great encouragement when it comes to planning. He shares, "The good news is that every minute spent in planning saves as many as ten minutes in execution. It takes only about ten to twelve minutes for you to plan out your day, but this small investment of time will save you up to two hours (100 to 120 minutes) in wasted time and diffused effort through the day."

Wow! Can you use an extra two hours? Sure! Planning will give you that opportunity.

Your project requires a significant amount of planning and preparation. So in this chapter, I'm going to give you some basic planning strategies. As you follow this approach, you will make significant progress in how successfully you are able to approach each day. In Chapters 6 and 7 you are going to learn a number of ways that you can specifically use your Transitional Time to meet your goals.

I encourage you to use S.M.A.A.R.T. goals. The acronym stands for Specific, Measurable, Achievable, Accountable, Relevant, and Time-bound. By utilizing this approach to writing out your goals, you will gain a lot of clarity and momentum. Let's consider how to apply each of these steps to your project, idea, book, etc., defined by your dream.

Don't become overwhelmed with the depth of this approach. You may think it is much too involved. Just remember, even though each area is somewhat detailed, I want you to be brief, but clear enough that it gives you direction. By following this approach, you will be well on your way to being able to use you Transitional Time to max out the profit of your investment.

Specific

The specific part of the goal looks at the What, When, Where, Who, Which, and Why. As you can see, it deals with the specifics, the details.

What defines your target. What are you doing? What are you trying to achieve with your project? What are your goals for that particular day or that particular event, so that you will clearly see what you are trying to accomplish? If I pick up your goal worksheet, I should be able to follow your thoughts easily.

When answers the timing question. When is the time frame that you desire to get this done? When do you need it done by? When do you expect to achieve this part of the plan? Knowing when helps you by allowing you to build a timeline by going to the end and working backward.

If you know that the project needs to be done six weeks from now, then put into play a six-week schedule, front-loaded instead of back-loaded. What I mean by that is, so many times people will have a project where they spend a large amount of time at the end pushing to get it finished. Try to front-load your project, because you never know what events are going to occur near the end of the process that are going to automatically add additional time to what you have to accomplish. By putting the bulk of the work at the beginning of the task, you can have time to be more creative near the end. Also, problems can be dealt with without excess stress.

Where identifies location. Where do you want to be or need to be in order to fulfill the goal?

Who answers the question of inclusion. Do you need a couple of people to help you achieve the goal, will you need a team of people, or will you be able to reach this goal alone? If you use other people, make sure you give the appropriate tasks to the right person. You don't want to have to spend a lot of time doing the task for someone else.

Which deals with the items that you will need. Which tools, resources, software, etc., do you need in order to successfully arrive at the outcome you desire? Not having the right tools is a huge waste of time.

When we lived in Zambia, Africa, the man who cut our yard took two days to do it with a six-inch single-sided swing blade. I purchased him a twelve-inch double-sided blade and reduced his time by an entire day. Later, I was able to get a push mower and he cut the yard in two hours. The right tool makes a lot of difference.

Why gives the reason. This area is one of the most important ones in the plan. Why are you even attempting this particular goal? The "Why" gives you the heart to keep going when things aren't going well. Many of the people that you will encounter may not understand the need for your project. Briefly defining the "Why" is helpful to you being able to help some people understand the importance of what you are providing. Ultimately, your desire is to help someone do something better, quicker, less costly, at a higher quality, etc. Your goal is about them.

Until they grasp the need, they will never understand *why* what you have is important. But the reverse is also true—once they discover the true value for themselves, they are sold. They will become your cheerleader and your best resource for new business. So, nail down the "Why" very clearly and your goal will push you forward.

Measurable

Specific goals are measurable. Determine how you will measure it. Will it be measured in time, space, quantity? Will it be financial, or will it be more subjective in the way that the measurement is made? Your project will determine that.

It is important to have a standardized measurement system, unless you are just using personal subjectivity as your measurement. Know what your beginning measurements are, so that you can compare accurately.

If your goal is to reach a certain level of sales by a certain date, that's very measurable. Saying you want to grow your company is not measurable. If you say you want to grow your company by 10 percent at the end of the next twelve months, that's very measurable.

Many people will talk about their company growth, church growth, or personal growth, when hard factual analysis shows no significant change. They didn't start with any analysis that told them where they were; therefore, everything that they consider growth is just subjective and it is also unprovable. Be detailed in your measurements. Start with real data and end with real data. Anything less than that and you will be cheating yourself, robbing yourself of the possibility of success.

Determining that you want to improve your product is a good goal. You can only reach it if you know the standards of the product already. If you want to improve a process or product or have specific things you want to improve, have customers verify whether or not that improvement is valid or have lab tests do that.

Achievable

Set a reachable goal. If goals are unreasonable and are missed normally, then you are setting a target that is too difficult. Regular failure will move you to abandon your goal and feel justified in doing so, when the reality was that the single step was too complex. Do not push yourself to meet one huge goal, but choose instead to reach several smaller goals.

Remember, you are working with Transitional Time to meet your goals. These are small amounts of time in which you will be dealing with very specific things. Attempt to break down your activities into smaller planning pieces than you may be encouraged to do in the normal work environment. Your target needs to be something that will challenge you and is valid.

Goals are intended to help you succeed. One after another, moving step by step, you want to be able to slowly and consistently progress through your goals. The size of your goal is not nearly as important as forward motion.

Accountable

Establish an approach to hold yourself accountable. As you move through your project plans, share each stage with an accountability partner. It is amazing how helpful and encouraging this person can be.

Choose a person who has an interest in a similar achievement. Set up a regularly scheduled checkpoint each week. The meeting can be a phone call or in person. Each week, set a goal and share what you desire to accomplish and report that to your partner. Share how well you did in reaching your goal, difficulties you encountered, surprises, etc. Allow them to ask some hard questions and hold yourself responsible to answer them honestly. Keep the checkup to about twenty to thirty minutes. A set time helps keep you focused and on track.

I have been amazed at how my accountability partners can spark my imagination by their comments and questions. Several times I have struggled in parts of a project and they have helped me through those spots, much more quickly than if I had not worked with them.

Relevant

Determine if a goal is relevant. Is what you are accomplishing closely connected or appropriate to the matter at hand? You may be able to achieve eight things in one day, but are each of them moving you toward your ultimate goal? If they are not, they're not relevant.

When you are working on a project, you can sometimes get sidetracked by pet project ideas—things that interest and excite you, ideas that entertain you, favorite "go-to" areas of thinking, and your natural strengths. It is easy to get distracted by these areas because they are fun or easy to work with.

However, the question is not whether you can accomplish something while thinking and working with your favorite areas, but whether you are diligently working on each of the areas that is relative to your project or your goal. Be careful not to just spin your wheels getting things done that don't apply. Or even repeating the same step over and over again. You're not really gaining ground if you are doing that.

Here are some suggested steps to test if something is relevant.

1. Is the item directly related to your project goal?
2. Is the item's completion vitally necessary for the goal to be met?
3. Using a scale of one to five, with one being the highest, rank the importance of this and other tasks to be completed in this stage of the project. Make sure you are staying focused on your project goal. Focus on the top priorities first.
4. If this part did not get done, how would it hurt the project? A low impact may show that this part is not relative.

Using the steps above, you can look at each part of your goal and determine whether it is something that is needed. If you find that the part is necessary to fulfill your project, then it is relative.

Time-bound

You need to set a deadline. Be realistic but push yourself. Also, pace yourself. For years I have wanted to complete a project like this and have failed. One of the reasons was that my time allotted was too long. I imagined that I had a whole year to write a book and I would never really be motivated by that deadline. Then I was challenged to write the book in thirty days. At first I laughed, never dreaming that it was even possible.

I found that placing myself under a shorter time restraint helped me to push through the project more quickly. My creativity seemed to flow better. I had to plan out the timing of each step and was more and more encouraged as I met each deadline.

As you set a deadline, and meet it, you will be encouraged too.

Now that you have a clear picture of S.M.A.A.R.T Goals, I would like for you to do two exercises. These practice sessions will help you understand how to apply that goal to yourself and your project.

S.M.A.A.R.T. Goals Guide

Taking the steps to develop S.M.A.A.R.T. Goals will help you know if a goal is realistic, reasonable, and relevant. It will also establish a real-time deadline. When writing S.M.A.A.R.T. Goals be brief and clear.

Use information that is important to understanding each step. Setting a good goal is the first step to success.

Initial Goal (write the original goal you are thinking about):

_____

_____

_____

_____

_____

1. Specific (What do you want to accomplish? Who needs to be included? When do you want to do this? Where do you want to do this? Which items need to be included? Why is this a goal?):

_____

_____

_____

_____

_____

2. Measurable (What measurement will you use to determine if you've successfully met your goal?):

_____

_____

_____

_____

_____

3. Achievable (Do you have or can you acquire the knowledge and skills required to achieve the goal in the time frame planned? Is the time frame realistic or does it need adjustment? Is the payback of reaching the goal worth the time and effort investment required?):

_____

_____

_____

_____

_____

4. Accountable (Who will be my accountability partner? When will I do my weekly checkup?):

_____

_____

_____

_____

_____

5. Relevant (Does this goal help me reach my final objective? Is this goal being attempted in the right order?):

_____

_____

_____

_____

_____

6. Time-bound (Is it actually possibly to reach the deadline?):

_____

_____

_____

_____

_____

New S.M.A.A.R.T. Goal (review what you have written, then write your new goal statement based on your answers to the previous questions):

_____

_____

_____

_____

_____

Daily Work Plan

Planning out how to think about your project during your day:

1. Review your Day Map and determine which parts of the day you will commit to your project. Take charge of your day and do not leave anything to chance.
2. Review your project plans, looking at the overall picture.
3. Review what you would like to focus on today.

4. Outline areas you need to think through or deal with in the day. (It amazes me when inspiration hits. The simplest things can spark ideas because I have outlined things to think about throughout the day.)

5. Ensure that you have some way to capture your thoughts and ideas (e.g., pen and paper, voice recorder, phone, computer, etc.).

6. Set aside a time at the end of your normal day where you can review what you were able to accomplish on that day and establish your priority for tomorrow.

Plan Even When Opportunity Doesn't Seem to Exist

Several years back, one of my friends developed a dream. He wanted to do something that was totally different than what he was trained to do and he began to use small amounts of time to develop his new company. Although there was actually no company in existence, it was in his head. Every spare moment, he planned little nuances of how he would run his new business.

One day, the company where he had worked for years announced it would merge with a larger company. For several months the merger process seemed positive and moved forward smoothly. One day, he and a number of other employees walked into their business only to discover that there were empty boxes sitting on their desks. They were all told to turn in their keys and fill their boxes with their personal items, then they were given severance checks. Panic set in. His whole team's job had been unexpectedly eliminated as a result of the merger.

He packed his box and walked to his car with his mind racing. What would he do next? How would he tell his wife that he had lost his job?

On his way home, he received a phone call from a person whom had been talking with him about the sideline business that he had a full plan in place to start. The caller wanted to know how he would develop certain a product line if he had the opportunity.

He quickly, clearly, and confidently shared with that person all the aspects of how that would work.

Planning had enabled him to give important details about the steps he would take. Before the call ended, he was asked how quickly he could provide a sample. He thought for a moment and gave a time.

The rest is history. On his way home, he went from being jobless to being the president of his own company. Literally, within just a few months, several of his products were a part of a nationwide release.

Planning met opportunity and the result was success!

What About You?

If you lost your job today, would you know enough about your dream that you could launch it into an income? What steps can you take that would ensure that you are prepared to take the next step?

The success of your dream depends on you. Take the opportunity to plan well and provide your dream the best start ever.

Intentionally set time aside to do important planning so you can capture the opportunity of the moment. Your Transitional Times allow you to keep things on your mind throughout the day.

Even while performing mundane tasks you will find that ideas will continually come across your mind. Often while reading there will be thoughts that help you understand how to approach something differently. Plan well. Grab the opportunity to direct your thinking so that it turns the routine into an opportunity for brilliance!

The Value of Planning

You really do save time by planning. Since time is your major obstacle to completing most of your tasks, you want to do everything you can to use it wisely. You will understand how invaluable your plans are as you begin to let them direct the usage of your daily Transitional Times.

Each day will already have a plan—or at least a piece of a plan—that will guide that day. Because you will be refreshing your thoughts on your plan constantly, don't worry if an idea hits you that is not in today's thought plan, yet is in the overall plan.

Run with the thought. Spend whatever time you need with the idea and file it away to use it at the appropriate time. It is always good to deal with the items in your plan as they come to mind. You will have the opportunity to put it all together later and it is easy to know where it fits—because you have a plan.

Wow! You have a dream! You have a plan! And, yes, you have time! With those three you are well on your way to achieving you goal. Now get ready to look at several ways you can invest in your time, specifically those small moments, and learn how they can produce a huge gain.

Chapter 6

Develop Transitional Time: Tools to Help Grow Your Time Investment Strategy

Are you ready to learn some specific ways that you can put your Transitional Time to work for you and make it more productive? In the next two chapters you will learn how to do just that. Some of the suggestions I will make will take more time than just five or ten minutes, but don't let that frustrate you. These are there to create the opportunities for you to be able to design how you can use your small amounts of time more effectively.

There is a big difference between *activity* and *accomplishment.* I want you to be able to move beyond just doing an activity to making that activity productive for you. Today, as you take charge of your Transitional Time, you are moving toward productivity and are on track to accomplish your dream.

A walk, drive, or ride to work is an activity. During the activity you move from one location to another. The goal has been met because you effectively arrived at work. But what did you personally accomplish? On the way to work did you listen to music, play a game, scream at crazy drivers, or daydream? You may have even done something extremely beneficial like listening to a motivational speaker, training audio, or audiobook. But again, what did you personally accomplish?

My goal with this question is to help you think differently. What can you do in your Transitional Times during the day that can help you reach the goals that you have in life? Instead of just going to work, make the ride to work *profitable*. Let's get going and learn specific ways that you can do just that.

Remember to take every opportunity that you can to use different approaches to help you come up with your ideas.

Outline Your Strategy

Strategize for progress. At the beginning of each week, take fifteen minutes and focus your attention to lay out what you would like to accomplish for that week. Don't spend your time on minute details, just put down the main points that you want to work with. If you want to only work with one point that whole week, that's okay, because it will probably have several different sub-points that develop as you move forward.

Whatever plan you decide to use to advance your goal is okay. The ultimate idea is to use your small amounts of time each day to make consistent progress. If one day you get the opportunity to actually write two or three thousand words about your project, that's great! Some days you may not even get two hundred words together—and that's okay too.

Reminder

Activities that can be considered Transitional Time: driving, riding the bus or subway, walking, waiting for an appointment, standing in the checkout line, dusting the house, cooking a meal (sometimes), showering, waiting on someone else to get ready, break time, a few minutes after your lunch break, etc.

Let me repeat:

Transitional Time is any time I am moving between two tasks and I personally have control of that time; when I am doing a routine task which does not require constant mental attention.

Time Investment Ledger

Track your time. Place your strategy and goal for the week at the top of the Time Investment Ledger. Determine how much time you plan to give your project this week. You can go back to your Day Map to see how much time that you can give.

If you can only put in ten minutes each day, then at the end of the week you would have put in seventy minutes. Remember you are not thinking about huge chunks of time. Think small segments. It is good if you can commit an hour or two, but you are looking for five, ten, twenty, or maybe even thirty minutes at a time. Once you begin your time investment plan, remember that it can be flexible so you can add to it at any time.

Be true to your commitment. A real investment will ensure success and an excellent return on your investment. Don't abandon your plan. If you miss completing a portion during one of the days, don't give up. Look back over your ledger and remember what you're trying to accomplish.

Utilize a notebook to keep a Time Investment Ledger. You can also download a template at www.timeinvestor.net look under the Tools category. Remember, this doesn't have to be anything fancy or time-consuming.

The goal of this ledger is very simple: to be an encouragement to you. When you look back at your ledger you will be amazed at how many segments of time you have filled with accomplishment. Keep the ledger very simple. Take a look at the example given in the ledger below.

Time Investment Ledger

Goal for the week: to develop a brochure that can help Customer Service deal with complaints and concerns by answering some of the recent issues about our product; can be used as a physical and/or e-brochure.

Transitional Activity	Normal Time	Invested Time	Accomplishment
1. Walk to work	12 minutes	8 minutes	Planned 2 steps of project.
2. Waiting at the doctor's office	20 minutes	15 minutes	Thought of three ways to answer a customer's question.
3. Shower	5 minutes	3 minutes	Developed brief outline for brochure.

Total Time Invested:	26 minutes
Most Significant Achievement:	Was able to deal successfully with a customer complaint by thinking through different approaches to their question.
Most Significant Result:	Retained a customer.

File a copy of your Time Investment Ledger and review them weekly and/or monthly to track your progress.

Idea Buckets

Create Idea Buckets either physically or electronically that will allow you to keep up with all your ideas. These "buckets" will allow you to access any of your thoughts at any time. So write, record, and file your thoughts.

Use as many bucket categories as you wish. As you begin to get more and more ideas, file them under similar areas of interest. Keep your thoughts; you will be able to refer back to them numerous times throughout the years as you think through other options to expand or improve your model.

When I started writing my first project, I thought, "How in the world can I get several chapters of information together for this?" Then I began collecting Idea Buckets, and over time ... It happened! Every time an idea would come to mind, I would write it or record it (everything I record is in a voice-to-text mode, so it is easy to send the note to myself and save them). Each new idea grew the project.

Don't dismiss anything. When you begin to think about your topic and write things down, don't leave out anything. Whatever comes to mind, put it down—you never know where a word or phrase will lead you. Some people are worried about not getting it right. The most important thing is to just get some things down on paper first. You can always go back and review everything you've done.

Remember, nothing is in concrete.

When you want to focus on an idea, get the bucket it is in, and spend your Transitional Time that day connecting, validating, or expanding the idea. Remember, this book is not just about time management, it is about helping you reach your dream.

Free to Change

When I started with this project I thought that I had several different options already nailed down as to how it would look. In my original process, I stuck pretty much to those ideas. As things progressed and I did different three-minute drills, I came up with several brand-new ideas. If you look at the project now versus what I had intended originally, you would find that it is probably about 80 percent different than the original project plan.

That's okay. It's my project. It's my dream.

It doesn't have to go according to the original plan. As I saw several of the new options, I began to realize that they were much more on target and went much better with what I was hoping or desiring than what I had originally planned. I believe that had I gone with my original thought it would have been good—but it wouldn't have been significant. It would have made some difference, but not *substantial* difference.

That's what you want: you desire the ability to fine-tune your project so that it can become substantial. You are not here just to throw an idea out. You want to make a huge impact on those who are around you. So don't dismiss ideas. They may contain the means by which you can influence change, grow your business, or write your book.

Start with a Problem to Solve

Start out a day with the thought, "What is the problem you want to solve?" During your Transitional Time work toward developing a solution. Start by thinking of questions you would ask about this problem. Ask others what their questions would be. Once you have come up with a list, assign one to each day over the course of two weeks.

This strategy will allow you to plan to look at different angles daily to solve the issue. Never assume that a problem has one side, or one way of looking at it. If you only see one approach, dig deeper.

Fifteen Questions for Entrepreneurs to Consider

As an Entrepreneur time is extremely valuable. Each moment affects income, growth, free time, etc. In thinking more along the business line of thought, here are some questions that can help stimulate your thinking:

1. What could someone improve upon that would make it hard for your business to compete?
2. What changes could you make that would allow you to be more relevant in a changing market?
3. Who can you partner with that you can add value to, and you can gain value from?
4. What are the fears which prevent you from making the changes that you feel can benefit you?
5. What segment of a problem do you see that is going unsolved?

6. If you did not create this business, what would your potential customers be missing?

7. What can you improve on in your product and customer service to produce a customer who eagerly recommends you to others?

8. Will your product fix a problem or fill a need?

9. Are you personally hearing input and feedback from a customer on a regular basis?

10. If a new leader were to take over your company, what would they do to improve it?

11. What are the three things your customers say they need?

12. If you had to say "no" to a customer, what can you do to be able to say "yes" the next time? Is that something you need to pursue?

13. How do you want your customers to improve as a result of your product?

14. If your success depends on the customer, how are you connecting with them to discover their needs?

15. What have you learned that you can teach others?

Using your Transitional Time, take one of these questions each day and spend your day wrestling with it. As you discover ways to answer these questions, you will discover the power that will revolutionize your business. Each of these answers have the potential to make you stronger, more competitive, and more applicable.

Eat Healthy

Ok, what does "eating healthy" have to do with effectively using your Transitional Time?

Eating healthy gives you the opportunity to think more clearly. Clear thinking is what gives you creativity. Do everything you can to assist yourself in achieving the goal that you have set out to achieve. During the moments that you have to focus your attention on your project you want to be able to productively think through it and be creative with every moment you have available.

I found this to be very true for me. Almost a decade ago, I was struggling to think through things as quickly or as focused as I used to be. You could even say that I was having "brain fog." Other than a stomach issue, I was very healthy. My doctor would soon discover that my issues for both my stomach and my mind were food allergies.

Once I discovered that, a simple but drastic alteration of my diet elevated my entire health and cleared up the issues with my mind. I could have never dreamed that a change of diet would alter my life so dramatically.

The confusion was not caused by age, intelligence, or lack of concentration. It was food. That may be true for some of you also. A change may allow you use your time better by being able to stay more focused, stay sharp longer, or become more creative.

Mental Block

Although every day offers a new opportunity, some days you just have a mental block. Developing your product or business plan or writing out your project occasionally gets stuck. Don't worry about it. Don't waste your time in *stuck mode*. Come back to it later in the day, or even the next day.

Don't allow frustration to stop you. When you experience those mental blocks, instead of being frustrated, go to something else. Read a related article, instruction guide, or the information that you added yesterday.

Sometimes I break the block by reading a paragraph from bottom to top. By focusing on each sentence in reverse order, it forces me to think outside the normal flow of thought. The result is that many times I can see things that I did not see earlier.

Change the scenery, walk to get a drink of water, exercise, or just try stretching. Many times just those few minutes away from the project allows you to see things differently.

It may be that you've spent too much time close up with the issue that you're dealing with. As my childhood physician used to tell me, sometimes you can't see the forest for the trees. He had a great little book that illustrated this very well.

It's also amazing what a good night's rest does to refresh your mind and give you a new insight into something. So don't fret. Look at a different piece of the project and move forward.

Dictionary Wordplay

A dictionary can be great to give you ideas, or even to deal with the mental blocks that you just read about. (Yes, an actual book, not online.) Set aside five to ten minutes and look in the dictionary at random words that you do not normally use and read through the meanings listed for each word. As you come across phrases or single words that spark ideas, write those down.

Sometimes you can do this even with words that you normally use. Look at the more complete definitions of that word. Many times we do not use a word in the same way that it is actually defined. As you discover their definitions, all of a sudden there's a spark of imagination resulting from the usage that we rarely see in conversation or writing.

You may not even use the word that sparks your imagination in what you are doing, but its value is in the fact that it gave you an idea. It's not the word that you are looking for necessarily—it is the spark. It is worth having a small pocket dictionary near you at all times and a large one at home. Short five-minute forays into the dictionary can produce dozens of hours of ideas to work through. It can also give you a clear point to focus on.

Step-by-Step

When thinking through a project, break it down into components that have an order. Then you can begin to write down the steps necessary to complete each phase and the total plan. Well-written instruction manuals can help you to think through a number of the steps you may want to take with your project.

As you plan out your day, you can take one step for each of your Transitional Times and think it through. Determine a point in each day that you will write down the steps that you developed throughout that day. As you review them, it is likely that you may think of one or two more steps that would help the process move more smoothly. You can think the question, Is a single step too complicated? If it is, insert another step or work to clarify the process better.

Over the period of the week, you can deal with many different parts in a process and make significant progress. Remember, little by little you reach your goal. Allow time for the small things to add up.

Know Your Audience

Knowing your audience will allow you to invest your time to do a better job in thinking a project through. Who are you targeting in providing your product or service? Are you targeting a fact-based person or someone who is more influenced by feeling? Do you need to engage facts, so that the intellect is answered, or do you need to provoke emotion, so that the feeling side is engaged? Certain projects may require that both fact and feeling are engaged.

Never underestimate your audience. Discover their needs, not your desired answer. So many times, I have watched people push the solutions to needs that they perceive without asking people what they need done. At the same time the people they are trying to help are resistant because they don't even sense that there is a need to begin with. As a result, the project lacks the ability to make the impact desired.

It is never a waste of time to discover what your audience needs or how they will react. Plan periods of time to interact with a variety of people and get their opinions. Opinions are always based on personal feeling—and even if they're missing the real need, don't discount what they are saying. The perception that they have is the only reality that you can work with, until you change their perception.

You and I need to be careful to engage people at a level that they can understand. We need to meet the needs that they actually have. You can do surveys. You can talk through things with folks over dinner. You can set up opportunities for people to share with you their needs. Go walking with a friend; engage in a conversation with a total stranger; ask questions that will allow you to understand your audience.

When your audience is not aware of the real need, help them understand. You may have heard that you can lead a horse to water but you can't make him drink. Well, ranchers have informed me that you can in fact *always* make a horse drink. You just have to give him some salt. Use your Transitional Time to develop ways to salt your audience so they need your information, product, or service.

Thesaurus

Looking up words in a thesaurus is similar to looking at the dictionary. Using this tool, you can find words that are similar but have different twists to what is being said. Sometimes, just seeing a single word that could replace a similar word or phrase can lead your thinking in a totally new direction.

What Have Others Done?

Your work does not have to reinvent the wheel. You can save a great deal of time by researching how others worked to handle a similar problem. You can utilize your public library. Also, there are many online resources—but whatever resources you use, make sure they are valid. There are a significant amount of resources both online and offline that are junk. In my own research, I regularly find bogus information.

If your project is a how-to, reading several articles or books that approach the subject from a how-to method will help you think through some of the necessary steps. The same would be true for sequential projects, coaching strategies, design layouts, or any other style that uses an approach similar to what you are trying to achieve.

Scan the table of contents and see what chapters may help you. Quickly—remember, this book does emphasize time management! —read through the chapter to see if you find anything of interest. Once you see the areas that apply, you can go back and reread that area later. By understanding how they move through their process successfully, it can help you move through your process.

If your project is highly technical, you can benefit by reading technical journals from those different areas you are planning on working with. If you just read a page or two of a journal during each of your break times, it would begin the process of learning and sparking your imagination.

Invest in your time wisely. Discovering a framework that helps you achieve your project goals is highly beneficial. That outline can save you many hours over the duration of your work on the venture.

Think Tank

Find a small group of people who are willing to hear out your project idea. Ask them to think of it from a critical viewpoint. They need to be thinking, Does the project idea flow well from point-to-point? Does it actually answer the questions being posed? Are there gaps that need to be addressed? and Are there any other significant issues discovered?

Get them to ask questions about your project. As you answer their questions, record the conversation. The questions they ask will help you think through the details necessary to clearly communicate your ideas to your intended audience. Think tanks are a great time investment.

The question-and-answer time doesn't need to be highly structured for it to be successful. It could be done over a coffee break or lunch time. You may even begin at a break one day and continue the questions and comments over several days. Allowing for these breaches in time will give you the opportunity to seriously consider several factors brought up by both the group asking you questions and the details of your responses.

You may also want to consider taking a small group out to eat to do this project. The meal would be part of their reward for participating in the discussion. When you get excellent information for the advancement of your project, you will count that as money well spent.

Take the information that you have learned and break it down into small bits. Then fit it into your Time Investment Ledger so that you can work on each part and develop it further. You will find that this can be invaluable to the success of your idea. Work hard at making your time work for you.

University Students

If you live near a college or university, you could get a group of students together that are in a field similar to the area you are working. Throw out your ideas to them and get them to brainstorm with you about how to develop your project.

If you are teaching students and you have the opportunity to assign research, you can do so related to your project. I had university professors that would do this and some finding in my research would spark an idea that would enable them to move forward with their own research.

Words of caution: two things. First, make sure that if you use someone else's research that you clear it with them and you give them credit. High integrity is important. Second, never blindly trust the research without completely checking the facts. If the research was faulty, then the credibility of your project would be highly compromised if you used it to back your theories.

I find that many students today rely simply on the Internet for their research. Encourage them to use source documents. As I mentioned earlier, many Internet "facts" do not go back to source documents and are in actual fact *false*. You want to be certain that your credibility remains intact. Therefore, use source documents to back up the research.

The questions, insights, and research of the students can provide you with many different ideas to consider in your Transitional Time. View this option as one that builds the opportunity for designing a roadmap to guide your thinking process later.

Trial Run

If the project you're working on is in a sequence, pick someone to do your project to discover how well they walk through the procedure. If in the process, you notice that they're struggling, you'll know to clarify the steps that need to be taken in order to complete the work. It is always good to have several people do a trial run. When choosing people to do your project, don't just choose people who are well-informed about that area.

You may want to choose someone that you know can follow instructions very well, someone who skims through instructions, and someone who seems to be oblivious to instructions altogether. If you can lead these three types of people through your project, you have an excellent opportunity at success as you learn how to provide the steps necessary for each one of these people to succeed in completing your sequence or project.

When you see them struggling, take note of that area. You should use your Transitional Time to work on a solution to the glitch that you discover. You may also want to consider how to approach the instructions to be clear from the viewpoint of people's different personalities. Accomplishing this can build more clarity and work to guarantee your success.

If/Then

Think about cause and effect. If *this* occurs, then *this* happens. Take your Transitional Times in the day and walk through each step of your project with the if/then idea.

Disassemble/Reassemble

If your project is one that is actually a physical product that can be disassembled, do it. While you are taking it apart, make notes of each step. You may even want to video this whole process and watch it later. As you see yourself doing something, more ideas are often generated. Are there any specific techniques needed to safely disassemble the product? Write them down.

Then reassemble the product. Again, write every step down. You may assume that because you wrote all the steps of disassembly down you don't necessarily need to do that for assembly. You do. The techniques of assembly and disassembly are many times significantly different. You may push a piece into place that latches in assembly but removing it would be significantly different.

Assign Transitional Times in the day to review the assembly and disassembly process. Never assume that anything is self-explanatory. Ask yourself if the instructions are clear, steps easily laid out, and if different personalities are taken into account? Walking through these steps will improve your instructions.

Before Going to the Next Chapter

Don't forget the significance of the Time Investment Ledger. It is highly valuable and encouraging as you look back and see your progress. You have a goal and you are going to accomplish it little by little.

In this chapter, you have looked at ten different ways that you can specifically use your time to positively impact the completion of your project. In the next chapter I will show you twelve more ways to utilize your time to make it work for you. As you invest in your time wisely, you will be gaining in knowledge, progressing toward your goal, and changing your life.

Remember, it does not take huge chunks of time—small amounts will do. And yes, you *do* have time. Now, let's look ahead and see some more opportunities to utilize your time for maximum benefit.

Chapter 7

Develop Transitional Time: Daily Investment Grows Your Impact

Remember, your goal is not just to be a better time manager. Your desire is to invest in your time wisely so that it works for you. As it becomes more productive, you are able to see your dreams become a reality.

As you go through your daily investment of time, how you think through your project is important. Make sure to review your real goal as you have defined it in your dream. In this chapter, you will continue to see different ways to think through your project so that you can come up with ways to effectively use the Transitional Time that you have available to you.

Remember to review your Day Map and your Time Investment Ledger. These two tools are highly important. They will help you discover your Transitional Times that you can use and they will help you track your progress. These two tools can be a great encouragement to you as you learn to effectively apply the ideas of both Chapters 6 and 7.

As you are moving forward in your project, I want to share with you a quote from Zig Ziglar that totally freed me up to be able to pursue my first project. Mr. Ziglar said, "If it's worth doing, it's worth doing poorly until you get it right."

Many people choose not to apply their time and effort to completing a project because they do not see themselves as being able to do it *well*. The fact is, no one can do it well to begin with. No sports star woke up one morning as a superstar. It took tremendous effort.

You have the dream. You have the time. Now continue to work on the skills that will allow you to utilize those small moments and produce huge benefits.

Simplicity

During your Transitional Times think through your project and ask yourself, How simple can I make a project? When you look through each of the steps, try and see if there are ways that you can make this simpler than it is right now. Boil it down to the smallest point. Make sure that you cover all the areas necessary, but make sure that you do that from a standpoint of being very basic or simplistic.

Try to reduce the steps to the least number possible. Make sure your instructions are very clear. Ask yourself if you would be able to hand your plan to someone who has no idea what you're doing and they would be able to follow it without your input.

Once you are certain that you have achieved your goal, allow someone else who knows nothing about your project to do it. If they struggle, you've got work to do. When they succeed, celebrate!

Develop Mini Plans

Sometimes projects are much larger. You struggle to get your mind around the total thing. That's okay. Again, break it into smaller pieces. As the adage goes, "How do you eat an elephant? One bite at a time."

Don't get caught up in seeing everything as being so overwhelming. Change how you view everything. Look at it as if you would a puzzle. Each project, goal, invention, etc., is just a group of small pieces. Break down the larger picture into those smaller pieces so that you are able to work on them in smaller amounts of time. Then develop the use of your time effectively.

Unplug

Yes, it is okay to relax!

Pressure builds up all around you; sometimes you are trying too hard and thinking too much about your plan. There are times that you need to just unplug. It's amazing that just being able to disconnect for a little while and walk away, thinking about nothing, can open up the ability to be more creative.

Don't stress yourself to the max. Make sure that you have the opportunity to focus on nothing at all for a little while. Get away from your computer, telephone, and interruptions of any kind and just spend time relaxing. It is okay, even necessary.

Remember, I have stated several times in this process that the goal is not to have every single moment of the day filled with activity. Your goal is simply to make progress. Small time investment by small time investment, you move forward. So, make sure that you include in your week times to relax.

Old School

Old can be new. Just because something is "old school" or original does not mean that it's invalid.

A number of years ago, I was watching as the medical profession was trying its best to defeat a rampant mutated bacterium that was seemingly unstoppable. Constantly they were coming up with new drugs, new ideas, and new theories on how to treat this viral strain.

One day, a researcher decided to do something just out of curiosity. He went back to the original drug that had been used to treat that bacterium many years earlier—the same drug that had become ineffective in treating the bacterium. However, in the process of continuing to change, the researcher discovered that the bacterium had become unprotected from the old drug again. The original drug worked and the bacterial rampage was stopped.

Sometimes you try to be creative, new, and fresh, and you may have failed to see the value in the old ways of doing something just because you have never seen them. There are many times that you personally can benefit in going back to the original way of looking at or doing something.

Do some research and see what was originally done that relates to your ideas. A foray into the past may launch your future. Yes, sometimes the old will still work. And remember, for many of the people, what is old is actually new—literally! They have no idea, because they have never seen it before.

So take some of your moments and take a trip to a museum, read historical accounts, discover architectural marvels, be amazed at how people with no technology were able to thrive. As you come away, look at how history can go to work for you.

Another Medium

If you've been verbally communicating something, write or draw it out. Come up with a song that says what you want to say. Develop a slideshow with pictures and ideas. Sometimes just getting into another medium will spark creativity.

About twenty years ago a friend of mine overheard his boss share concerns about how to accomplish a task. After thinking about it for several weeks, he came up with a possible solution to the problem. He then invited his boss out to lunch so that he could tell him what he was thinking.

His approach was pretty well-thought-out, but incomplete. There were still a couple of sticking points that he was trying to work through, but he felt confident that he could share the information well enough to be understood. So, well prepared, he took the risk.

As they were at lunch he wanted to make the presentation as clear as possible, so he decided to draw it out, literally. He picked up a napkin and began to draw his plan. Surprisingly to him, as he drew, the steps that he was struggling with suddenly became clear. As a result, he was assigned the duty of writing out the details and overseeing the project.

During your Transitional Times, take the opportunity to develop something that deals with your project from a different approach. Create a form, develop the ideas for a slideshow, draw out a logo, etc., to put your project in a different medium and allow your mind to become more creative in how it approaches a solution.

Fill the Void

In thinking through your ideas, use questions like these to help you. What do people want that they don't currently have? What kind of opportunity would they like? What do they desire to be different? What help are they asking for that there's currently no solution? In the answers to these questions you will find opportunity. Come up with articles, inventions, projects, etc., that would allow you the ability to meet those needs.

Always be attentive and watch people. It will not take you long, when asking the right types of questions, to become aware of a need. Once the need is discovered, develop a solution to meet it.

How are you thinking through your project? Is it moving you toward being productive? Is it leading you to fill the void? Make sure your time is being used productively. Wisely invested time can help you discover the issues that you need to focus on to be highly effective.

Break the Norm

Break the norm. Do something differently. If you usually write, plan, or develop your strategy in the same way or at the same place all the time, try using a different location.

Changing from an easy chair to a writing desk or a formal dining table can actually help you be more creative. I was amazed when I found out that something this simple could completely reignite my ability to think through a project clearly. So, if you're having a mental block doing it one way you have the freedom to do it another way.

You may want to move outdoors to a picnic table or go to a park. There may be times that you will even want to go to a place that's crowded. Go to a mall or a subway station, sit in a spot or lean against a wall, and think through your project.

One good thing about using your Transitional Time is that it usually puts you in multiple locations automatically (subway, car, walking, etc.). Don't rule any one of those locations out as being a good opportunity. You may think that a packed subway car is not a good place. I have found that when I force myself to use my time productively, even in awkward places, I sometimes am more creative. Don't worry what others will think—just focus on your goal.

Don't sit at stuck very long. Make a change so that you can invest the moments that you have effectively.

Acronyms and Word Games

I like acronyms. I like the challenge of building a series of words off of letters that support my idea. Sometimes to build the acronym it requires getting out the dictionary or the thesaurus. Sticking with the word I am building an acronym from limits my choices and therefore forces me to think in a different way. When I force myself to come up with a word for each letter that helps me toward solving my problem, it always seems to help.

Another thing that I do is play word games. Sometimes these games are simply comparing one word to another. Also, you can try playing words against each other as opposites. At another time you could just simply try to come up with synonyms. Anything that helps you discover new thoughts, directions, or ideas to help you reach your goal is beneficial.

You can use your Transitional Time very easily to do acronyms and word games. Although they are simple and fun activities they are keeping you engaged in the thought process of moving you towards your dream.

Plan, Produce, Payoff—Board

Place a whiteboard or a corkboard somewhere in your home where you will be able to see it every day.

Put the title of your project at the top and do a simple outline of your project on the board. As part of your daily routine, check on where you are in the progress toward your goal each day. Choose an area to focus on for the day.

Throughout the day, think of ideas related to the part of the project that you wanted to focus on today. Make sure you record your ideas. When you get home, write the information on the board or pin your notes on the board in the place where they properly belong.

If you want to do this electronically there are a number of ways to do this. You can use a cloud based product that will allow you to make notes from any device. These notes can be placed in the file as your Transitional Times are happening. At the end of each day you can print out your thought and add them to your physical board.

The physical board provides a great visual example of your progress and it allows you to see everything at one time. Here you can really see small amounts of information add up. Can you imagine going from a blank board to a board with thirty different ideas of how to approach something or complete areas that have tremendous amounts of information in just a few weeks? When you look at that board and see all those ideas, it will energize you to go further. The board will also allow you to clearly see in a tangible way that your Transitional Time is paying off for you.

Involve the whole family. Give them an opportunity to see what is going on. They can become your cheerleaders. Also, give them permission to put ideas on your board. The synergy that begins to come, because of the collaboration, will have an even more dramatic impact.

If two brothers or sisters or a husband and wife wanted to collaborate on a project, this would give them a great tool to do so. Sometimes personal schedules do not allow a lot of time together, but the board will help keep things progressing.

The board helps you plan and produce, and leads to a great payoff. It keeps the thought process fresh and current even though you may not be able to personally talk with the other person every day in any detail about the project. I would put this board close to the door you most often go in and out or in a common area that you will definitely see every day.

If you have placed your outline in any detail on the board then it can help you, as you leave the house, to be reminded of where your thoughts need to track that day. The more easily that information can be made available, the more likely you are to take the opportunity to use it.

You may decide that one week, all you want to focus on is one specific area of the project or chapter of the book. In as much detail as you can, place the outline of information that you're wanting to deal with, during that week, on your board. Now everyone who sees the board is focused on one area.

Everyone can be a part of the progress. More small moments are piling up to create a massive amount of information and opportunity.

Arrive Early

Some of you leave early for work on a regular basis because of traffic or other issues. On some days you end up getting to work fifteen to twenty minutes early. What if instead of going on and clocking in, you took that extra fifteen minutes and use them as Transitional Time (at least occasionally) and dedicate that time toward your goal?

Some people use this time to build relationships with coworkers. Relationships are powerful and important. I would never ask you to give them up totally, nor for long periods. But what if you took just a fraction of that time and dedicated it to your project, and then the rest of the time to your relationships?

By letting your coworkers know that you have a project that you are working on, and for the next two weeks that will be your focus, they will understand that you are not just avoiding them. Doing this for a set time frame can benefit you greatly. Even those little changes will make a huge impact as you move forward.

Creative People

Surround yourself with creative people. Jim Rohn says, "You are the average of the five people you spend the most time with." Make sure that those five people are among the brightest, most intelligent, most energetic, and most desirous to get something done. These people can become some of the greatest encouragers in your life.

A number of years ago I decided to intentionally include these kinds of people in my friendships. Some of the people I wanted to include, I knew it would be difficult because of their schedules. I also didn't know if they would even take time to spend with me. But I had to take the risk.

I began to read their books and listen to their audio recordings and webinars. Then I started to attend conferences with which they would be involved. Later, we had the opportunity to meet in person. I've been amazed how many of these people are truly interested in personally helping people improve. Some of them actually took the time to be with me and to influence me. Direct connection created positive influences.

I remember the very first time that I got brave enough to go up to one of the conference speakers and just simply say I would like to build a personal relationship with him. He was open to that, but I could tell he thought nothing would ever come of it. So much of the time, people do not follow through with their desires because of fear.

On a monthly basis, I began to contact him by phone. Each time I called, I would have notes in front of me from the previous call that I had reviewed. I also had prepared one or two questions that I was hoping to get his input or advice on. I knew he didn't have much time and I respected that by being prepared and brief.

After the call was over, I would write an email to him letting him know how much I appreciated the moments that he had given me. I would always add at least one significant thing I have learned from our brief conversation that day.

Those small investments of time have proved to be some of the most encouraging things that have ever occurred in my life. Over time some of these relationships blossomed into true friendships.

Don't assume that busy people have no time for you. Respect them and their busy schedule, but still take the risk and invite them to be a part of your life.

Could you take fifteen minutes a month and dedicate it to getting to know some of the brightest minds in your area of interest? It could turn into genuine relationships and deep friendships. It may be the most important fifteen minutes you ever spend in a month. Take the risk—it's worth it.

Voice-to-Text

My most used tool is voice-to-text. I struggle with typing, and I don't like to take a long period of time to write a large volume of things on paper. So much of what I do is voice-to-text. There is some excellent software out there that allows you to do this easily and accurately.

You don't have to spend a large amount of money to have some of the best software available. Some word processing software already comes with a version of that capability built in. So take advantage of being able to talk out what you're wanting to say.

One of the things that I've done in years past is carry on a conversation with myself, in front of a mirror, about what I'm trying to do. Literally, I would act as if I were carrying on a conversation with someone else. These conversations were always recorded so that I would have a record of my responses. I would use questions that are similar to many of the exercises that you have been using throughout this book.

Thoughts could freely flow as my mind would deal with different angles and ideas. Many times thoughts will come to mind that I have not had earlier and had not planned to say. The fact that I was doing it "talk-to-text" also allowed me to email the final notes to myself. Sometimes I was directly recording to my computer.

I know that this may be uncomfortable for some of you at first. Some people like to think through every step first before they say anything. Do an experiment. Outline a brief idea and then talk it out. I think you will be amazed at what you can accomplish.

Take advantage of every opportunity to utilize your time. Many times, you can speak thoughts more rapidly than you can write. In this regard, voice-to-text is an amazing time investment.

Invest and Reap

Each of the actions in these last two chapters are here to help you invest your time wisely in your project. Choose several of these approaches to help you complete your project well. Give yourself every opportunity to succeed!

A good investment in your time will pay off in multiple ways. I look forward to seeing your reward!

Chapter 8

Rewards of Time Investment

You have been through a significant process. These exercises were challenging and they led you to clearly understand your dreams and goals. Now it is impossible to look back and see everything in the same light as before.

With your dream in focus, plans made, and time redefined, you are ready to move forward. Each step of the process has its own rewards. You are benefiting from them each time you make them a part of your daily life.

Let's take a moment and recognize the rewards you gain as you move through each step.

#1—Time Redefined

You see time as an investment.

You now know that time is not something to spend, waste, endure, or watch go by. It is an investment! This new perspective makes you see every moment as important. You desire to claim the energy of each minute because you know that no moment can be reclaimed. It's not like money that can be made and lost and remade. Time is more valuable.

Because you have changed the way you look at time, you have time to transform your life. Now you see the value of time and understand the necessity of making a major investment in it.

You know that you have the same amount of time as everybody else. Time is the one area in which no one has an advantage. It is *use it or lose it*. As you invest well, your investment will pay off in huge ways.

The area where you have learned to invest in differently is your Transitional Time. You discovered that these small amounts of time are valuable and under your control.

Let's look at the definition one more time.

Transitional Time is any time I am moving between two tasks and I personally have control of that time; when I am doing a routine task which does not require constant mental attention.

Your use of Transitional Time is now able to revolutionize your life and the life of your family. Dormant thoughts can come to life. Your Transitional Time is now ready to be invested wisely! You will be greatly rewarded by this new view.

#2—Time Debits Neutralized

You are in control of time debits and are turning them into credits!

Being aware of the time debits and knowing how to turn them into credits now gives you more time. You are in more control of your time. Interruptions do not dominate your day. Time debits are no longer preventing you from being productive. Quick effective action is allowing you to remove or reduce time debits.

Anger, worry, perfectionism, unpreparedness, etc., are now re-channeled into areas of productivity. You are giving your work all the time it requires and doing your very best. Because you're more effective at your workplace, you have gained more time to personally control.

In your personal time, you are not letting time wasters be in control. Meeting your goals takes precedence over gaming, social media, and other time debits. Yes, you are going to have times where you plan to have fun and relax. No stressing out! But your dream now sets the priorities.

You are now able to position yourself to reach your goals and ultimately your dream. Your life is looking different. You are more energized. You're grasping more opportunity. Time investments are placing credits in your life. These credits are a great reward and give you more time.

#3—The Great Time Discovery

You really do have time!

Wow! You discovered that you have more time available to put toward your dream than you ever thought. What a rewarding find!

Also, you discovered the amazing ability of what you can do in a ten-minute period. Through that discovery, you learned that you can accomplish a great goal in small amounts of time. Large quantities of time are not always necessary to reach every goal.

Look, huge blocks of time are not necessary to be effective when you are investing in your life. Small consistent time investments add up to great profits.

You discovered that using Transitional Times can produce powerful achievements. What you saw was the entire idea behind this project—to use small moments for huge gains. By getting this far, I know that you're the type of person that is ready to invest in time well!

As you progress, you have the opportunity of going back and doing your Day Map over and over again. And you should! You can discover new time opportunities. Anytime your life schedule changes, redo your Day Map. You can now capture the power of the small moments! Soon you will see the rewards of ten minute segments invested wisely piling up!

#4—Defined Dreams

You now have a well-defined dream!

Your dream is your future. Under time debits, you learned that the greatest time waster was the failure to have a defined dream. But you are not dreamless. You never were. You may not have been able to define it completely, but you definitely weren't *dreamless*. The fact that you bought this book shows that.

You now have developed or rethought your personal dream. It has been reviewed, refined, and launched or relaunched! The dream is now clear and is guiding you to where you want to be.

Go back and refresh your dream often. Remember, in my story I had a dream and lived it, but then I lost the dream. By refreshing your dream, you can review and rethink the process and keep the fire kindled. It is easier to walk through that process as you're still moving with momentum than to try and redirect things when you come to a complete stop.

Your defined dream now gives you a clear path for progress. You are on your way to achieving your goals. You are now investing your time in things that matter to you! Your defined dream will reward you daily.

#5—Planned Progress

You have a plan.

Plans are putting your dreams within reach. The S.M.A.A.R.T. planning approach is saving you time, ensuring your time is productive, and reducing your stress. Your strategy is giving your dream real substance. The skeleton of the plan is beginning to allow muscles and flesh to be visible on your project.

With a plan, each day is productive because you are proactive. You're able to break down the most complicated and challenging issues into small enough pieces to be accomplished.

Perfectionism does not stop you.

Although to be perfect is your goal, you are not worried if it is not perfect the first time. Remember what Zig Ziglar said: "Anything worth doing is worth doing poorly until you can do it right."

You are not overwhelmed.

You can break big tasks into small pieces. The elephant is not so overwhelming because you are choosing to eat it bite by bite. You are planning, getting better at breaking it down into goals, and accomplishing more.

You are investing small amounts of time consistently to give the result of huge gains. Planning gives the small moments meaning and give you tremendous rewards when you invest in them.

#6—Creativity Meets Opportunity

You are making Transitional Time count!

You are using some of the strategies revealed in chapters 6 and 7 and investing in time for the greatest benefits. You are choosing those approaches that best fit your goal and making the most of it.

You recognize the value of small things.

No idea is thrown away. They are recorded and kept in Idea Buckets for future use. The creative opportunities will arise to allow you to use the information. Having these thoughts to help will allow you to develop future projects faster and more completely.

You think through projects from different angles to improve their development.

You see questions as desirable and helpful aids in developing your project. You do drills on how to do step-by-step processing or even create trial runs of your project. Several different approaches are used during your Transitional Time to improve developing your opportunities. Instead of seeing a question as negative, you are using it as a launch pad to improvement.

You are encouraged by your progress.

The Time Investment Ledger is a valuable tool for encouragement. The ledger is allowing you to have an ongoing record of the value of your time investment. By using it you are seeing a clear picture of how your small amounts of time are transforming your life.

Celebrate the building of your life's dream as you review a stack of time investments. There is a great amount of joy in accomplishing a task.

These eleven rewards will work to make your life focused and fulfilled. Recognize them for the power they truly have to encourage you in meeting your dreams.

Now What?

So here you are. Another book read. Another idea considered. But where do you go from here?

My goal was not just to try and motivate you and encourage you, or to keep you studying about something. Motivation has its place and should be a part of everyone's life. We desperately need it.

My goal is to get you productive. Productivity is the greatest motivator. Having your name attached to something of value, where you put in your sweat equity, thoughts, and research to produce a tool, product, or procedure that is able to change your part of the world—*that* is highly motivating.

My goal through this whole book has been to help you understand that you have time to get it done and give you some practical ways to use that time. The small moments you discovered, wisely invested, will produce huge gains. I can't wait to see the results of what you accomplish through investing in your time.

Yes, You Can Do It!

You can do it! No matter how large or complicated your project or task is, *You Can Do It!* The ability, tools, and opportunity are all available. Now, as a result of your efficient time investment, the time you need is also available.

By following the procedure you have just read, you will gain significant time to invest in your own life. You are the best judge of how to invest in yourself. Others will not be focused on investing in you. By taking control of your time, others will be unable to rob you of your time.

Use your Transitional Time to make a difference for yourself. As you improve your skills as a time investor, your life will improve and so will those around you.

Stop! Don't worry about what others think about your dream. The success of your project lies within you. You need to be living your dream. What everyone else thinks your dream should be is not the most important thing. God made you as a unique individual and He wants you to fulfill the dream He placed in your heart and mind. Go full steam ahead and achieve it!

As I've stated several times through the process, if you have someone who raises serious questions about your dream, consider those questions and address valid issues. But I can share this with you: most of the questions offered by "Dream Killers" will be invalid. Do not spend your time dealing with irrelevant questions.

Produce a workable plan. It gives you an opportunity to save time, stay focused, and move forward. Your plan gives detail for your day and guides you to success! Invest in your time wisely. Time is life.

Sharing Your Success With Others

Let me hear about your successes as you invest in your time. I would like to know what goal you set and how long it took you to get there. Would you also be willing to share what you learned along the way?

You can come and be a part of a community that is wanting to encourage others to be excellent time investors, just like you are becoming. You can inspire others and get encouragement yourself by sharing with us your success at www.timeinvestor.net. Let others join in celebrating the progress that you are making.

Share your success of a discovered dream, successful planning, a product launch, or a completed project. Each success will be unique to the dream it is attached too. No two dreams are alike and every dream is important.

Whatever your success, I want to be able to celebrate it with you. I want others to be able to come along and encourage you, help you through challenges, and see you through steps that lead to accomplishment.

By succeeding together, each person grows, encourages, and strengthens. Take the opportunity to be a part of helping someone else. Zig Ziglar always said, "You can have everything in life that you want if you will just help enough other people get what they want."

Remember that. Helping others allows us to be successful.

Through allowing me to share your personal success, you will help others solve problems, create opportunities, invent products, and overcome boundaries. The possibilities are limitless.

So take the next step. With your established dream, plan your work and work on your plan day by day. Reach your goals bit by bit. Increase your productivity. Soon you will discover how much the pursuit of this project has changed your life.

Results

You are reading the results of the effective use of Transitional Time. Investing wisely in your Transitional Time can be powerful. You can fine-tune your dream. In addition, develop and tweak plans to realize your goal.

I had a dream and was able to see it to completion as a result of using my Transitional Time. More than 70 percent of the information you have just read was either transcribed, dreamed, or thought through during my own personal Transitional Time.

You are reading a direct testament of the use of Transitional Time. I didn't have time to sit down and write up all the things that were necessary in order for me to think through this project. I couldn't carve major periods of time out of my busy schedule. But I was able to repurpose time. On my way to and from work, between business appointments or events, or waiting for an appointment, I was working through this project and the content for the website, www.timeinvestor.net.

It is amazing to me to see all that has been possible. I could not have foreseen the results. A simple ten-minute exercise changed everything for me. My personal thoughts had been that I didn't have time. That was true—under the definition of time as I had perceived it. As I began to see even small segments of time as an investment, I began to look for the possible payoff that could come from that venture. After all, no one invests unless there's a possibility for significant returns.

The completion of this book is part of my payback. I've achieved one of my goals. I did it without having to produce more time in my day. I invested in the time I already had.

Now it is your turn!

Produce your product, book, project, invention, etc. Take the opportunity to influence lives. Move beyond the excuse of being too busy and not having enough time, and invest in the time you have. Become a producer. Be a problem solver. Help people to grow. Make a positive impact.

You can do it! You have the time to do it! Focus on investing in your small moments to make huge gains!

One last time, together:

"Yes, I do have time!"

Acknowledgments

Every person has special individuals in their life that have made significant impacts. Over the years, I can look back and see many teachers and leaders who have impacted my life. Pastors like Jim Akins, JV Reeves, Bobby Welch, and Rob Zinn, have been great friends and spiritual leaders along this path.

My university and seminary professors Bob Agee, James Eaves, David Irby, Alva Parks, Leon Marsh, and many others, led me to believe that there are no unsolvable problems, the Bible is true, and God is always with us.

Some specific business leaders that have been a major part of encouraging me have been Zig Ziglar, Tom Ziglar, Dan Miller, Howard Partridge, Michael Hyatt, Dave Anderson and Jonathan Milligan. These are a few people who have made a huge impact on my life and have helped me to say, "Yes, I do have time to do this project."

Thank you for being my mentors, encouragers, and friends.

About the Author

Dr. James "Butch" Tanner and his wife Carole have two grown daughters. Currently, he and his wife live in Hong Kong. He has over 40 years of experience in leading churches and teams of people. He has worked with paid and volunteer staffs to lead churches to restructure, re-dream, and find their potential. Dr. Tanner is aware of the challenges of new things. He has led his congregations to help start 21 new churches and many new ministries. Constant changes and the 24/7 nature of ministry have created many opportunities to develop time management skills. The demands of new ventures and large memberships have equipped him to address the area of time investment. He also has lived and worked in the United States and Zambia Africa.

www.ingramcontent.com/pod-product-compliance
Lightning Source LLC
La Vergne TN
LVHW051234080426
835513LV00016B/1587